C-4694   CAREER EXAMINATION SERIES

This is your
PASSBOOK for...

MDS/Nurse Assessment Coordinator

Test Preparation Study Guide
Questions & Answers

COPYRIGHT NOTICE

This book is SOLELY intended for, is sold ONLY to, and its use is RESTRICTED to individual, bona fide applicants or candidates who qualify by virtue of having seriously filed applications for appropriate license, certificate, professional and/or promotional advancement, higher school matriculation, scholarship, or other legitimate requirements of education and/or governmental authorities.

This book is NOT intended for use, class instruction, tutoring, training, duplication, copying, reprinting, excerption, or adaptation, etc., by:

1) Other publishers
2) Proprietors and/or Instructors of "Coaching" and/or Preparatory Courses
3) Personnel and/or Training Divisions of commercial, industrial, and governmental organizations
4) Schools, colleges, or universities and/or their departments and staffs, including teachers and other personnel
5) Testing Agencies or Bureaus
6) Study groups which seek by the purchase of a single volume to copy and/or duplicate and/or adapt this material for use by the group as a whole without having purchased individual volumes for each of the members of the group
7) Et al.

Such persons would be in violation of appropriate Federal and State statutes.

PROVISION OF LICENSING AGREEMENTS – Recognized educational, commercial, industrial, and governmental institutions and organizations, and others legitimately engaged in educational pursuits, including training, testing, and measurement activities, may address request for a licensing agreement to the copyright owners, who will determine whether, and under what conditions, including fees and charges, the materials in this book may be used them. In other words, a licensing facility exists for the legitimate use of the material in this book on other than an individual basis. However, it is asseverated and affirmed here that the material in this book CANNOT be used without the receipt of the express permission of such a licensing agreement from the Publishers. Inquiries re licensing should be addressed to the company, attention rights and permissions department.

All rights reserved, including the right of reproduction in whole or in part, in any form or by any means, electronic or mechanical, including photocopying, recording, or by any information storage and retrieval system, without permission in writing from the Publisher.

Copyright © 2024 by
National Learning Corporation

212 Michael Drive, Syosset, NY 11791
(516) 921-8888 • www.passbooks.com
E-mail: info@passbooks.com

PUBLISHED IN THE UNITED STATES OF AMERICA

PASSBOOK® SERIES

THE *PASSBOOK® SERIES* has been created to prepare applicants and candidates for the ultimate academic battlefield – the examination room.

At some time in our lives, each and every one of us may be required to take an examination – for validation, matriculation, admission, qualification, registration, certification, or licensure.

Based on the assumption that every applicant or candidate has met the basic formal educational standards, has taken the required number of courses, and read the necessary texts, the *PASSBOOK® SERIES* furnishes the one special preparation which may assure passing with confidence, instead of failing with insecurity. Examination questions – together with answers – are furnished as the basic vehicle for study so that the mysteries of the examination and its compounding difficulties may be eliminated or diminished by a sure method.

This book is meant to help you pass your examination provided that you qualify and are serious in your objective.

The entire field is reviewed through the huge store of content information which is succinctly presented through a provocative and challenging approach – the question-and-answer method.

A climate of success is established by furnishing the correct answers at the end of each test.

You soon learn to recognize types of questions, forms of questions, and patterns of questioning. You may even begin to anticipate expected outcomes.

You perceive that many questions are repeated or adapted so that you can gain acute insights, which may enable you to score many sure points.

You learn how to confront new questions, or types of questions, and to attack them confidently and work out the correct answers.

You note objectives and emphases, and recognize pitfalls and dangers, so that you may make positive educational adjustments.

Moreover, you are kept fully informed in relation to new concepts, methods, practices, and directions in the field.

You discover that you are actually taking the examination all the time: you are preparing for the examination by "taking" an examination, not by reading extraneous and/or supererogatory textbooks.

In short, this PASSBOOK®, used directedly, should be an important factor in helping you to pass your test.

MDS/NURSE ASSESSMENT COORDINATOR

The American Association of Nurse Assessment Coordination (AANAC) defines a nurse assessment coordinator (NAC) as the nurse who is accountable for coordinating and overseeing the full collaborative, interdisciplinary assessment and care planning process in skilled nursing facilities. This process includes comprehensive resident assessments; care coordination and planning; resident advocacy and teaching; facilitation of open communication among care team members, the resident, and family; collection and transmission of data for the purposes of quality improvement; and adherence to the Minimum Data Set (MDS) and Resident Assessment Instrument (RAI) requirements. The ultimate goal of the assessment and care planning process is to promote the resident's quality of care and life in a skilled nursing facility, including individuality, safety, wellness, satisfaction, and dignity.

This position involves the responsibility for assessing and evaluating residents for coverage. The incumbent is responsible for a case mix with emphasis on meeting or exceeding budget expectations. The work is performed under the supervision of nursing home administrator and the director of nursing with leeway given for carrying out the details of the work. Does related work as required.

The job responsibilities are at the discretion of the employer and could include any number of duties. CMS requires that a registered nurse serve in a coordinating role for the RAI process, with the responsibility of signing off on completion of the document.

The position is generally referred to as "MDS coordinator," as the role requires an understanding of MDS 3.0 and RAI rules and regulations. The job requires nursing assessment skills and the ability to conceive and create care plans based on a comprehensive resident assessment that is accomplished through resident and family interviews, physical assessment, observation, and input from the care team. Nurse Practice Acts indicate variation in the role of registered nurses (RNs) and licensed practical nurses (LPNs) for nursing assessment; however, federal regulations related to the RAI clearly define what components of assessment should be addressed for persons admitted to nursing homes and the ongoing clinical decision making that is within the scope of practice of RNs but not LPNs. It is not unusual for facility administrators to hire an LPN to fulfill the responsibilities of the NAC, under the supervision of an RN.

SUBJECTS OF EXAMINATION:
The written test is designed to evaluate knowledge, skills, and/or abilities in the following areas:
1. **Evaluating health care** - These questions will test for knowledge in areas such as: content of medical records; criteria for admissions, services, and continued stays; treatment and discharge planning process; alternate care determinations and community resources; utilization review and quality management concepts and process.
2. **Medical, psychiatric, developmental conditions and treatments** - These questions will test for knowledge in areas such as: acceptable treatments and standard medical alternatives; symptoms, tests, procedures, and treatments associated with specific diagnoses; evaluation of the appropriateness of treatment methods; characteristics of the various populations diagnosed with mental illness or intellectual/developmental disabilities.
3. **Preparing written material** - These questions test for the ability to present information clearly and accurately, and to organize paragraphs logically and comprehensibly. For some questions, you will be given information in two or three sentences followed by four restatements of the information. You must then choose the best version. For other questions, you will be given paragraphs with their sentences out of order. You must then choose, from four suggestions, the best order for the sentences.
4. **Understanding and interpreting written material** - These questions test how well you comprehend written material. You will be provided with brief reading selections and will be asked questions about the selections. All the information required to answer the questions will be presented in the selections; you will not be required to have any special knowledge relating to the subject areas of the selections.

HOW TO TAKE A TEST

I. YOU MUST PASS AN EXAMINATION

A. WHAT EVERY CANDIDATE SHOULD KNOW

Examination applicants often ask us for help in preparing for the written test. What can I study in advance? What kinds of questions will be asked? How will the test be given? How will the papers be graded?

As an applicant for a civil service examination, you may be wondering about some of these things. Our purpose here is to suggest effective methods of advance study and to describe civil service examinations.

Your chances for success on this examination can be increased if you know how to prepare. Those "pre-examination jitters" can be reduced if you know what to expect. You can even experience an adventure in good citizenship if you know why civil service exams are given.

B. WHY ARE CIVIL SERVICE EXAMINATIONS GIVEN?

Civil service examinations are important to you in two ways. As a citizen, you want public jobs filled by employees who know how to do their work. As a job seeker, you want a fair chance to compete for that job on an equal footing with other candidates. The best-known means of accomplishing this two-fold goal is the competitive examination.

Exams are widely publicized throughout the nation. They may be administered for jobs in federal, state, city, municipal, town or village governments or agencies.

Any citizen may apply, with some limitations, such as the age or residence of applicants. Your experience and education may be reviewed to see whether you meet the requirements for the particular examination. When these requirements exist, they are reasonable and applied consistently to all applicants. Thus, a competitive examination may cause you some uneasiness now, but it is your privilege and safeguard.

C. HOW ARE CIVIL SERVICE EXAMS DEVELOPED?

Examinations are carefully written by trained technicians who are specialists in the field known as "psychological measurement," in consultation with recognized authorities in the field of work that the test will cover. These experts recommend the subject matter areas or skills to be tested; only those knowledges or skills important to your success on the job are included. The most reliable books and source materials available are used as references. Together, the experts and technicians judge the difficulty level of the questions.

Test technicians know how to phrase questions so that the problem is clearly stated. Their ethics do not permit "trick" or "catch" questions. Questions may have been tried out on sample groups, or subjected to statistical analysis, to determine their usefulness.

Written tests are often used in combination with performance tests, ratings of training and experience, and oral interviews. All of these measures combine to form the best-known means of finding the right person for the right job.

II. HOW TO PASS THE WRITTEN TEST

A. NATURE OF THE EXAMINATION

To prepare intelligently for civil service examinations, you should know how they differ from school examinations you have taken. In school you were assigned certain definite pages to read or subjects to cover. The examination questions were quite detailed and usually emphasized memory. Civil service exams, on the other hand, try to discover your present ability to perform the duties of a position, plus your potentiality to learn these duties. In other words, a civil service exam attempts to predict how successful you will be. Questions cover such a broad area that they cannot be as minute and detailed as school exam questions.

In the public service similar kinds of work, or positions, are grouped together in one "class." This process is known as *position-classification*. All the positions in a class are paid according to the salary range for that class. One class title covers all of these positions, and they are all tested by the same examination.

B. FOUR BASIC STEPS

1) Study the announcement

How, then, can you know what subjects to study? Our best answer is: "Learn as much as possible about the class of positions for which you've applied." The exam will test the knowledge, skills and abilities needed to do the work.

Your most valuable source of information about the position you want is the official exam announcement. This announcement lists the training and experience qualifications. Check these standards and apply only if you come reasonably close to meeting them.

The brief description of the position in the examination announcement offers some clues to the subjects which will be tested. Think about the job itself. Review the duties in your mind. Can you perform them, or are there some in which you are rusty? Fill in the blank spots in your preparation.

Many jurisdictions preview the written test in the exam announcement by including a section called "Knowledge and Abilities Required," "Scope of the Examination," or some similar heading. Here you will find out specifically what fields will be tested.

2) Review your own background

Once you learn in general what the position is all about, and what you need to know to do the work, ask yourself which subjects you already know fairly well and which need improvement. You may wonder whether to concentrate on improving your strong areas or on building some background in your fields of weakness. When the announcement has specified "some knowledge" or "considerable knowledge," or has used adjectives like "beginning principles of..." or "advanced ... methods," you can get a clue as to the number and difficulty of questions to be asked in any given field. More questions, and hence broader coverage, would be included for those subjects which are more important in the work. Now weigh your strengths and weaknesses against the job requirements and prepare accordingly.

3) Determine the level of the position

Another way to tell how intensively you should prepare is to understand the level of the job for which you are applying. Is it the entering level? In other words, is this the position in which beginners in a field of work are hired? Or is it an intermediate or advanced level? Sometimes this is indicated by such words as "Junior" or "Senior" in the class title. Other jurisdictions use Roman numerals to designate the level – Clerk I, Clerk II, for example. The word "Supervisor" sometimes appears in the title. If the level is not indicated by the title, check the description of duties. Will you be working under very close supervision, or will you have responsibility for independent decisions in this work?

4) Choose appropriate study materials

Now that you know the subjects to be examined and the relative amount of each subject to be covered, you can choose suitable study materials. For beginning level jobs, or even advanced ones, if you have a pronounced weakness in some aspect of your training, read a modern, standard textbook in that field. Be sure it is up to date and has general coverage. Such books are normally available at your library, and the librarian will be glad to help you locate one. For entry-level positions, questions of appropriate difficulty are chosen – neither highly advanced questions, nor those too simple. Such questions require careful thought but not advanced training.

If the position for which you are applying is technical or advanced, you will read more advanced, specialized material. If you are already familiar with the basic principles of your field, elementary textbooks would waste your time. Concentrate on advanced textbooks and technical periodicals. Think through the concepts and review difficult problems in your field.

These are all general sources. You can get more ideas on your own initiative, following these leads. For example, training manuals and publications of the government agency which employs workers in your field can be useful, particularly for technical and professional positions. A letter or visit to the government department involved may result in more specific study suggestions, and certainly will provide you with a more definite idea of the exact nature of the position you are seeking.

III. KINDS OF TESTS

Tests are used for purposes other than measuring knowledge and ability to perform specified duties. For some positions, it is equally important to test ability to make adjustments to new situations or to profit from training. In others, basic mental abilities not dependent on information are essential. Questions which test these things may not appear as pertinent to the duties of the position as those which test for knowledge and information. Yet they are often highly important parts of a fair examination. For very general questions, it is almost impossible to help you direct your study efforts. What we can do is to point out some of the more common of these general abilities needed in public service positions and describe some typical questions.

1) General information

Broad, general information has been found useful for predicting job success in some kinds of work. This is tested in a variety of ways, from vocabulary lists to questions about current events. Basic background in some field of work, such as sociology or economics, may be sampled in a group of questions. Often these are principles which have become familiar to most persons through exposure rather than through formal training. It is difficult to advise you how to study for these questions; being alert to the world around you is our best suggestion.

2) Verbal ability

An example of an ability needed in many positions is verbal or language ability. Verbal ability is, in brief, the ability to use and understand words. Vocabulary and grammar tests are typical measures of this ability. Reading comprehension or paragraph interpretation questions are common in many kinds of civil service tests. You are given a paragraph of written material and asked to find its central meaning.

3) Numerical ability

Number skills can be tested by the familiar arithmetic problem, by checking paired lists of numbers to see which are alike and which are different, or by interpreting charts and graphs. In the latter test, a graph may be printed in the test booklet which you are asked to use as the basis for answering questions.

4) Observation

A popular test for law-enforcement positions is the observation test. A picture is shown to you for several minutes, then taken away. Questions about the picture test your ability to observe both details and larger elements.

5) Following directions

In many positions in the public service, the employee must be able to carry out written instructions dependably and accurately. You may be given a chart with several columns, each column listing a variety of information. The questions require you to carry out directions involving the information given in the chart.

6) Skills and aptitudes

Performance tests effectively measure some manual skills and aptitudes. When the skill is one in which you are trained, such as typing or shorthand, you can practice. These tests are often very much like those given in business school or high school courses. For many of the other skills and aptitudes, however, no short-time preparation can be made. Skills and abilities natural to you or that you have developed throughout your lifetime are being tested.

Many of the general questions just described provide all the data needed to answer the questions and ask you to use your reasoning ability to find the answers. Your best preparation for these tests, as well as for tests of facts and ideas, is to be at your physical and mental best. You, no doubt, have your own methods of getting into an exam-taking mood and keeping "in shape." The next section lists some ideas on this subject.

IV. KINDS OF QUESTIONS

Only rarely is the "essay" question, which you answer in narrative form, used in civil service tests. Civil service tests are usually of the short-answer type. Full instructions for answering these questions will be given to you at the examination. But in case this is your first experience with short-answer questions and separate answer sheets, here is what you need to know:

1) Multiple-choice Questions

Most popular of the short-answer questions is the "multiple choice" or "best answer" question. It can be used, for example, to test for factual knowledge, ability to solve problems or judgment in meeting situations found at work.

A multiple-choice question is normally one of three types—
- It can begin with an incomplete statement followed by several possible endings. You are to find the one ending which *best* completes the statement, although some of the others may not be entirely wrong.
- It can also be a complete statement in the form of a question which is answered by choosing one of the statements listed.

- It can be in the form of a problem – again you select the best answer.

Here is an example of a multiple-choice question with a discussion which should give you some clues as to the method for choosing the right answer:

When an employee has a complaint about his assignment, the action which will *best* help him overcome his difficulty is to
- A. discuss his difficulty with his coworkers
- B. take the problem to the head of the organization
- C. take the problem to the person who gave him the assignment
- D. say nothing to anyone about his complaint

In answering this question, you should study each of the choices to find which is best. Consider choice "A" – Certainly an employee may discuss his complaint with fellow employees, but no change or improvement can result, and the complaint remains unresolved. Choice "B" is a poor choice since the head of the organization probably does not know what assignment you have been given, and taking your problem to him is known as "going over the head" of the supervisor. The supervisor, or person who made the assignment, is the person who can clarify it or correct any injustice. Choice "C" is, therefore, correct. To say nothing, as in choice "D," is unwise. Supervisors have and interest in knowing the problems employees are facing, and the employee is seeking a solution to his problem.

2) True/False Questions

The "true/false" or "right/wrong" form of question is sometimes used. Here a complete statement is given. Your job is to decide whether the statement is right or wrong.

SAMPLE: A roaming cell-phone call to a nearby city costs less than a non-roaming call to a distant city.

This statement is wrong, or false, since roaming calls are more expensive.

This is not a complete list of all possible question forms, although most of the others are variations of these common types. You will always get complete directions for answering questions. Be sure you understand *how* to mark your answers – ask questions until you do.

V. RECORDING YOUR ANSWERS

Computer terminals are used more and more today for many different kinds of exams.

For an examination with very few applicants, you may be told to record your answers in the test booklet itself. Separate answer sheets are much more common. If this separate answer sheet is to be scored by machine – and this is often the case – it is highly important that you mark your answers correctly in order to get credit.

An electronic scoring machine is often used in civil service offices because of the speed with which papers can be scored. Machine-scored answer sheets must be marked with a pencil, which will be given to you. This pencil has a high graphite content which responds to the electronic scoring machine. As a matter of fact, stray dots may register as answers, so do not let your pencil rest on the answer sheet while you are pondering the correct answer. Also, if your pencil lead breaks or is otherwise defective, ask for another.

Since the answer sheet will be dropped in a slot in the scoring machine, be careful not to bend the corners or get the paper crumpled.

The answer sheet normally has five vertical columns of numbers, with 30 numbers to a column. These numbers correspond to the question numbers in your test booklet. After each number, going across the page are four or five pairs of dotted lines. These short dotted lines have small letters or numbers above them. The first two pairs may also have a "T" or "F" above the letters. This indicates that the first two pairs only are to be used if the questions are of the true-false type. If the questions are multiple choice, disregard the "T" and "F" and pay attention only to the small letters or numbers.

Answer your questions in the manner of the sample that follows:

32. The largest city in the United States is
   A. Washington, D.C.
   B. New York City
   C. Chicago
   D. Detroit
   E. San Francisco

1) Choose the answer you think is best. (New York City is the largest, so "B" is correct.)
2) Find the row of dotted lines numbered the same as the question you are answering. (Find row number 32)
3) Find the pair of dotted lines corresponding to the answer. (Find the pair of lines under the mark "B.")
4) Make a solid black mark between the dotted lines.

VI. BEFORE THE TEST

Common sense will help you find procedures to follow to get ready for an examination. Too many of us, however, overlook these sensible measures. Indeed, nervousness and fatigue have been found to be the most serious reasons why applicants fail to do their best on civil service tests. Here is a list of reminders:

- Begin your preparation early – Don't wait until the last minute to go scurrying around for books and materials or to find out what the position is all about.
- Prepare continuously – An hour a night for a week is better than an all-night cram session. This has been definitely established. What is more, a night a week for a month will return better dividends than crowding your study into a shorter period of time.
- Locate the place of the exam – You have been sent a notice telling you when and where to report for the examination. If the location is in a different town or otherwise unfamiliar to you, it would be well to inquire the best route and learn something about the building.
- Relax the night before the test – Allow your mind to rest. Do not study at all that night. Plan some mild recreation or diversion; then go to bed early and get a good night's sleep.
- Get up early enough to make a leisurely trip to the place for the test – This way unforeseen events, traffic snarls, unfamiliar buildings, etc. will not upset you.
- Dress comfortably – A written test is not a fashion show. You will be known by number and not by name, so wear something comfortable.

- Leave excess paraphernalia at home – Shopping bags and odd bundles will get in your way. You need bring only the items mentioned in the official notice you received; usually everything you need is provided. Do not bring reference books to the exam. They will only confuse those last minutes and be taken away from you when in the test room.
- Arrive somewhat ahead of time – If because of transportation schedules you must get there very early, bring a newspaper or magazine to take your mind off yourself while waiting.
- Locate the examination room – When you have found the proper room, you will be directed to the seat or part of the room where you will sit. Sometimes you are given a sheet of instructions to read while you are waiting. Do not fill out any forms until you are told to do so; just read them and be prepared.
- Relax and prepare to listen to the instructions
- If you have any physical problem that may keep you from doing your best, be sure to tell the test administrator. If you are sick or in poor health, you really cannot do your best on the exam. You can come back and take the test some other time.

VII. AT THE TEST

The day of the test is here and you have the test booklet in your hand. The temptation to get going is very strong. Caution! There is more to success than knowing the right answers. You must know how to identify your papers and understand variations in the type of short-answer question used in this particular examination. Follow these suggestions for maximum results from your efforts:

1) Cooperate with the monitor

The test administrator has a duty to create a situation in which you can be as much at ease as possible. He will give instructions, tell you when to begin, check to see that you are marking your answer sheet correctly, and so on. He is not there to guard you, although he will see that your competitors do not take unfair advantage. He wants to help you do your best.

2) Listen to all instructions

Don't jump the gun! Wait until you understand all directions. In most civil service tests you get more time than you need to answer the questions. So don't be in a hurry. Read each word of instructions until you clearly understand the meaning. Study the examples, listen to all announcements and follow directions. Ask questions if you do not understand what to do.

3) Identify your papers

Civil service exams are usually identified by number only. You will be assigned a number; you must not put your name on your test papers. Be sure to copy your number correctly. Since more than one exam may be given, copy your exact examination title.

4) Plan your time

Unless you are told that a test is a "speed" or "rate of work" test, speed itself is usually not important. Time enough to answer all the questions will be provided, but this does not mean that you have all day. An overall time limit has been set. Divide the total time (in minutes) by the number of questions to determine the approximate time you have for each question.

5) Do not linger over difficult questions

If you come across a difficult question, mark it with a paper clip (useful to have along) and come back to it when you have been through the booklet. One caution if you do this – be sure to skip a number on your answer sheet as well. Check often to be sure that you have not lost your place and that you are marking in the row numbered the same as the question you are answering.

6) Read the questions

Be sure you know what the question asks! Many capable people are unsuccessful because they failed to *read* the questions correctly.

7) Answer all questions

Unless you have been instructed that a penalty will be deducted for incorrect answers, it is better to guess than to omit a question.

8) Speed tests

It is often better NOT to guess on speed tests. It has been found that on timed tests people are tempted to spend the last few seconds before time is called in marking answers at random – without even reading them – in the hope of picking up a few extra points. To discourage this practice, the instructions may warn you that your score will be "corrected" for guessing. That is, a penalty will be applied. The incorrect answers will be deducted from the correct ones, or some other penalty formula will be used.

9) Review your answers

If you finish before time is called, go back to the questions you guessed or omitted to give them further thought. Review other answers if you have time.

10) Return your test materials

If you are ready to leave before others have finished or time is called, take ALL your materials to the monitor and leave quietly. Never take any test material with you. The monitor can discover whose papers are not complete, and taking a test booklet may be grounds for disqualification.

VIII. EXAMINATION TECHNIQUES

1) Read the general instructions carefully. These are usually printed on the first page of the exam booklet. As a rule, these instructions refer to the timing of the examination; the fact that you should not start work until the signal and must stop work at a signal, etc. If there are any *special* instructions, such as a choice of questions to be answered, make sure that you note this instruction carefully.

2) When you are ready to start work on the examination, that is as soon as the signal has been given, read the instructions to each question booklet, underline any key words or phrases, such as *least, best, outline, describe* and the like. In this way you will tend to answer as requested rather than discover on reviewing your paper that you *listed without describing*, that you selected the *worst* choice rather than the *best* choice, etc.

3) If the examination is of the objective or multiple-choice type – that is, each question will also give a series of possible answers: A, B, C or D, and you are called upon to select the best answer and write the letter next to that answer on your answer paper – it is advisable to start answering each question in turn. There may be anywhere from 50 to 100 such questions in the three or four hours allotted and you can see how much time would be taken if you read through all the questions before beginning to answer any. Furthermore, if you come across a question or group of questions which you know would be difficult to answer, it would undoubtedly affect your handling of all the other questions.

4) If the examination is of the essay type and contains but a few questions, it is a moot point as to whether you should read all the questions before starting to answer any one. Of course, if you are given a choice – say five out of seven and the like – then it is essential to read all the questions so you can eliminate the two that are most difficult. If, however, you are asked to answer all the questions, there may be danger in trying to answer the easiest one first because you may find that you will spend too much time on it. The best technique is to answer the first question, then proceed to the second, etc.

5) Time your answers. Before the exam begins, write down the time it started, then add the time allowed for the examination and write down the time it must be completed, then divide the time available somewhat as follows:
    - If 3-1/2 hours are allowed, that would be 210 minutes. If you have 80 objective-type questions, that would be an average of 2-1/2 minutes per question. Allow yourself no more than 2 minutes per question, or a total of 160 minutes, which will permit about 50 minutes to review.
    - If for the time allotment of 210 minutes there are 7 essay questions to answer, that would average about 30 minutes a question. Give yourself only 25 minutes per question so that you have about 35 minutes to review.

6) The most important instruction is to *read each question* and make sure you know what is wanted. The second most important instruction is to *time yourself properly* so that you answer every question. The third most important instruction is to *answer every question*. Guess if you have to but include something for each question. Remember that you will receive no credit for a blank and will probably receive some credit if you write something in answer to an essay question. If you guess a letter – say "B" for a multiple-choice question – you may have guessed right. If you leave a blank as an answer to a multiple-choice question, the examiners may respect your feelings but it will not add a point to your score. Some exams may penalize you for wrong answers, so in such cases *only*, you may not want to guess unless you have some basis for your answer.

7) Suggestions
    a. Objective-type questions
        1. Examine the question booklet for proper sequence of pages and questions
        2. Read all instructions carefully
        3. Skip any question which seems too difficult; return to it after all other questions have been answered
        4. Apportion your time properly; do not spend too much time on any single question or group of questions

5. Note and underline key words – *all, most, fewest, least, best, worst, same, opposite,* etc.
6. Pay particular attention to negatives
7. Note unusual option, e.g., unduly long, short, complex, different or similar in content to the body of the question
8. Observe the use of "hedging" words – *probably, may, most likely,* etc.
9. Make sure that your answer is put next to the same number as the question
10. Do not second-guess unless you have good reason to believe the second answer is definitely more correct
11. Cross out original answer if you decide another answer is more accurate; do not erase until you are ready to hand your paper in
12. Answer all questions; guess unless instructed otherwise
13. Leave time for review

  b. Essay questions
     1. Read each question carefully
     2. Determine exactly what is wanted. Underline key words or phrases.
     3. Decide on outline or paragraph answer
     4. Include many different points and elements unless asked to develop any one or two points or elements
     5. Show impartiality by giving pros and cons unless directed to select one side only
     6. Make and write down any assumptions you find necessary to answer the questions
     7. Watch your English, grammar, punctuation and choice of words
     8. Time your answers; don't crowd material

8) Answering the essay question

Most essay questions can be answered by framing the specific response around several key words or ideas. Here are a few such key words or ideas:

M's: manpower, materials, methods, money, management
P's: purpose, program, policy, plan, procedure, practice, problems, pitfalls, personnel, public relations

  a. Six basic steps in handling problems:
     1. Preliminary plan and background development
     2. Collect information, data and facts
     3. Analyze and interpret information, data and facts
     4. Analyze and develop solutions as well as make recommendations
     5. Prepare report and sell recommendations
     6. Install recommendations and follow up effectiveness

  b. Pitfalls to avoid
     1. *Taking things for granted* – A statement of the situation does not necessarily imply that each of the elements is necessarily true; for example, a complaint may be invalid and biased so that all that can be taken for granted is that a complaint has been registered

2. *Considering only one side of a situation* – Wherever possible, indicate several alternatives and then point out the reasons you selected the best one
3. *Failing to indicate follow up* – Whenever your answer indicates action on your part, make certain that you will take proper follow-up action to see how successful your recommendations, procedures or actions turn out to be
4. *Taking too long in answering any single question* – Remember to time your answers properly

IX. AFTER THE TEST

Scoring procedures differ in detail among civil service jurisdictions although the general principles are the same. Whether the papers are hand-scored or graded by machine we have described, they are nearly always graded by number. That is, the person who marks the paper knows only the number – never the name – of the applicant. Not until all the papers have been graded will they be matched with names. If other tests, such as training and experience or oral interview ratings have been given, scores will be combined. Different parts of the examination usually have different weights. For example, the written test might count 60 percent of the final grade, and a rating of training and experience 40 percent. In many jurisdictions, veterans will have a certain number of points added to their grades.

After the final grade has been determined, the names are placed in grade order and an eligible list is established. There are various methods for resolving ties between those who get the same final grade – probably the most common is to place first the name of the person whose application was received first. Job offers are made from the eligible list in the order the names appear on it. You will be notified of your grade and your rank as soon as all these computations have been made. This will be done as rapidly as possible.

People who are found to meet the requirements in the announcement are called "eligibles." Their names are put on a list of eligible candidates. An eligible's chances of getting a job depend on how high he stands on this list and how fast agencies are filling jobs from the list.

When a job is to be filled from a list of eligibles, the agency asks for the names of people on the list of eligibles for that job. When the civil service commission receives this request, it sends to the agency the names of the three people highest on this list. Or, if the job to be filled has specialized requirements, the office sends the agency the names of the top three persons who meet these requirements from the general list.

The appointing officer makes a choice from among the three people whose names were sent to him. If the selected person accepts the appointment, the names of the others are put back on the list to be considered for future openings.

That is the rule in hiring from all kinds of eligible lists, whether they are for typist, carpenter, chemist, or something else. For every vacancy, the appointing officer has his choice of any one of the top three eligibles on the list. This explains why the person whose name is on top of the list sometimes does not get an appointment when some of the persons lower on the list do. If the appointing officer chooses the second or third eligible, the No. 1 eligible does not get a job at once, but stays on the list until he is appointed or the list is terminated.

X. HOW TO PASS THE INTERVIEW TEST

The examination for which you applied requires an oral interview test. You have already taken the written test and you are now being called for the interview test – the final part of the formal examination.

You may think that it is not possible to prepare for an interview test and that there are no procedures to follow during an interview. Our purpose is to point out some things you can do in advance that will help you and some good rules to follow and pitfalls to avoid while you are being interviewed.

What is an interview supposed to test?

The written examination is designed to test the technical knowledge and competence of the candidate; the oral is designed to evaluate intangible qualities, not readily measured otherwise, and to establish a list showing the relative fitness of each candidate – as measured against his competitors – for the position sought. Scoring is not on the basis of "right" and "wrong," but on a sliding scale of values ranging from "not passable" to "outstanding." As a matter of fact, it is possible to achieve a relatively low score without a single "incorrect" answer because of evident weakness in the qualities being measured.

Occasionally, an examination may consist entirely of an oral test – either an individual or a group oral. In such cases, information is sought concerning the technical knowledges and abilities of the candidate, since there has been no written examination for this purpose. More commonly, however, an oral test is used to supplement a written examination.

Who conducts interviews?

The composition of oral boards varies among different jurisdictions. In nearly all, a representative of the personnel department serves as chairman. One of the members of the board may be a representative of the department in which the candidate would work. In some cases, "outside experts" are used, and, frequently, a businessman or some other representative of the general public is asked to serve. Labor and management or other special groups may be represented. The aim is to secure the services of experts in the appropriate field.

However the board is composed, it is a good idea (and not at all improper or unethical) to ascertain in advance of the interview who the members are and what groups they represent. When you are introduced to them, you will have some idea of their backgrounds and interests, and at least you will not stutter and stammer over their names.

What should be done before the interview?

While knowledge about the board members is useful and takes some of the surprise element out of the interview, there is other preparation which is more substantive. It *is* possible to prepare for an oral interview – in several ways:

1) Keep a copy of your application and review it carefully before the interview

This may be the only document before the oral board, and the starting point of the interview. Know what education and experience you have listed there, and the sequence and dates of all of it. Sometimes the board will ask you to review the highlights of your experience for them; you should not have to hem and haw doing it.

2) Study the class specification and the examination announcement

Usually, the oral board has one or both of these to guide them. The qualities, characteristics or knowledges required by the position sought are stated in these documents. They offer valuable clues as to the nature of the oral interview. For example, if the job involves supervisory responsibilities, the announcement will usually indicate that knowledge of modern supervisory methods and the qualifications of the candidate as a supervisor will be tested. If so, you can expect such questions, frequently in the form of a hypothetical situation which you are expected to solve. NEVER go into an oral without knowledge of the duties and responsibilities of the job you seek.

3) Think through each qualification required

Try to visualize the kind of questions you would ask if you were a board member. How well could you answer them? Try especially to appraise your own knowledge and background in each area, *measured against the job sought*, and identify any areas in which you are weak. Be critical and realistic – do not flatter yourself.

4) Do some general reading in areas in which you feel you may be weak

For example, if the job involves supervision and your past experience has NOT, some general reading in supervisory methods and practices, particularly in the field of human relations, might be useful. Do NOT study agency procedures or detailed manuals. The oral board will be testing your understanding and capacity, not your memory.

5) Get a good night's sleep and watch your general health and mental attitude

You will want a clear head at the interview. Take care of a cold or any other minor ailment, and of course, no hangovers.

What should be done on the day of the interview?

Now comes the day of the interview itself. Give yourself plenty of time to get there. Plan to arrive somewhat ahead of the scheduled time, particularly if your appointment is in the fore part of the day. If a previous candidate fails to appear, the board might be ready for you a bit early. By early afternoon an oral board is almost invariably behind schedule if there are many candidates, and you may have to wait. Take along a book or magazine to read, or your application to review, but leave any extraneous material in the waiting room when you go in for your interview. In any event, relax and compose yourself.

The matter of dress is important. The board is forming impressions about you – from your experience, your manners, your attitude, and your appearance. Give your personal appearance careful attention. Dress your best, but not your flashiest. Choose conservative, appropriate clothing, and be sure it is immaculate. This is a business interview, and your appearance should indicate that you regard it as such. Besides, being well groomed and properly dressed will help boost your confidence.

Sooner or later, someone will call your name and escort you into the interview room. *This is it.* From here on you are on your own. It is too late for any more preparation. But remember, you asked for this opportunity to prove your fitness, and you are here because your request was granted.

What happens when you go in?

The usual sequence of events will be as follows: The clerk (who is often the board stenographer) will introduce you to the chairman of the oral board, who will introduce you to the other members of the board. Acknowledge the introductions before you sit down. Do not be surprised if you find a microphone facing you or a stenotypist sitting by. Oral interviews are usually recorded in the event of an appeal or other review.

Usually the chairman of the board will open the interview by reviewing the highlights of your education and work experience from your application – primarily for the benefit of the other members of the board, as well as to get the material into the record. Do not interrupt or comment unless there is an error or significant misinterpretation; if that is the case, do not hesitate. But do not quibble about insignificant matters. Also, he will usually ask you some question about your education, experience or your present job – partly to get you to start talking and to establish the interviewing "rapport." He may start the actual questioning, or turn it over to one of the other members. Frequently, each member undertakes the questioning on a particular area, one in which he is perhaps most competent, so you can expect each member to participate in the examination. Because time is limited, you may also expect some rather abrupt switches in the direction the questioning takes, so do not be upset by it. Normally, a board member will not pursue a single line of questioning unless he discovers a particular strength or weakness.

After each member has participated, the chairman will usually ask whether any member has any further questions, then will ask you if you have anything you wish to add. Unless you are expecting this question, it may floor you. Worse, it may start you off on an extended, extemporaneous speech. The board is not usually seeking more information. The question is principally to offer you a last opportunity to present further qualifications or to indicate that you have nothing to add. So, if you feel that a significant qualification or characteristic has been overlooked, it is proper to point it out in a sentence or so. Do not compliment the board on the thoroughness of their examination – they have been sketchy, and you know it. If you wish, merely say, "No thank you, I have nothing further to add." This is a point where you can "talk yourself out" of a good impression or fail to present an important bit of information. Remember, *you close the interview yourself.*

The chairman will then say, "That is all, Mr. _____, thank you." Do not be startled; the interview is over, and quicker than you think. Thank him, gather your belongings and take your leave. Save your sigh of relief for the other side of the door.

How to put your best foot forward

Throughout this entire process, you may feel that the board individually and collectively is trying to pierce your defenses, seek out your hidden weaknesses and embarrass and confuse you. Actually, this is not true. They are obliged to make an appraisal of your qualifications for the job you are seeking, and they want to see you in your best light. Remember, they must interview all candidates and a non-cooperative candidate may become a failure in spite of their best efforts to bring out his qualifications. Here are 15 suggestions that will help you:

1) Be natural – Keep your attitude confident, not cocky

If you are not confident that you can do the job, do not expect the board to be. Do not apologize for your weaknesses, try to bring out your strong points. The board is interested in a positive, not negative, presentation. Cockiness will antagonize any board member and make him wonder if you are covering up a weakness by a false show of strength.

2) Get comfortable, but don't lounge or sprawl

Sit erectly but not stiffly. A careless posture may lead the board to conclude that you are careless in other things, or at least that you are not impressed by the importance of the occasion. Either conclusion is natural, even if incorrect. Do not fuss with your clothing, a pencil or an ashtray. Your hands may occasionally be useful to emphasize a point; do not let them become a point of distraction.

3) Do not wisecrack or make small talk

This is a serious situation, and your attitude should show that you consider it as such. Further, the time of the board is limited – they do not want to waste it, and neither should you.

4) Do not exaggerate your experience or abilities

In the first place, from information in the application or other interviews and sources, the board may know more about you than you think. Secondly, you probably will not get away with it. An experienced board is rather adept at spotting such a situation, so do not take the chance.

5) If you know a board member, do not make a point of it, yet do not hide it

Certainly you are not fooling him, and probably not the other members of the board. Do not try to take advantage of your acquaintanceship – it will probably do you little good.

6) Do not dominate the interview

Let the board do that. They will give you the clues – do not assume that you have to do all the talking. Realize that the board has a number of questions to ask you, and do not try to take up all the interview time by showing off your extensive knowledge of the answer to the first one.

7) Be attentive

You only have 20 minutes or so, and you should keep your attention at its sharpest throughout. When a member is addressing a problem or question to you, give him your undivided attention. Address your reply principally to him, but do not exclude the other board members.

8) Do not interrupt

A board member may be stating a problem for you to analyze. He will ask you a question when the time comes. Let him state the problem, and wait for the question.

9) Make sure you understand the question

Do not try to answer until you are sure what the question is. If it is not clear, restate it in your own words or ask the board member to clarify it for you. However, do not haggle about minor elements.

10) Reply promptly but not hastily

A common entry on oral board rating sheets is "candidate responded readily," or "candidate hesitated in replies." Respond as promptly and quickly as you can, but do not jump to a hasty, ill-considered answer.

11) Do not be peremptory in your answers

A brief answer is proper – but do not fire your answer back. That is a losing game from your point of view. The board member can probably ask questions much faster than you can answer them.

12) Do not try to create the answer you think the board member wants

He is interested in what kind of mind you have and how it works – not in playing games. Furthermore, he can usually spot this practice and will actually grade you down on it.

13) Do not switch sides in your reply merely to agree with a board member

Frequently, a member will take a contrary position merely to draw you out and to see if you are willing and able to defend your point of view. Do not start a debate, yet do not surrender a good position. If a position is worth taking, it is worth defending.

14) Do not be afraid to admit an error in judgment if you are shown to be wrong

The board knows that you are forced to reply without any opportunity for careful consideration. Your answer may be demonstrably wrong. If so, admit it and get on with the interview.

15) Do not dwell at length on your present job

The opening question may relate to your present assignment. Answer the question but do not go into an extended discussion. You are being examined for a *new* job, not your present one. As a matter of fact, try to phrase ALL your answers in terms of the job for which you are being examined.

Basis of Rating

Probably you will forget most of these "do's" and "don'ts" when you walk into the oral interview room. Even remembering them all will not ensure you a passing grade. Perhaps you did not have the qualifications in the first place. But remembering them will help you to put your best foot forward, without treading on the toes of the board members.

Rumor and popular opinion to the contrary notwithstanding, an oral board wants you to make the best appearance possible. They know you are under pressure – but they also want to see how you respond to it as a guide to what your reaction would be under the pressures of the job you seek. They will be influenced by the degree of poise you display, the personal traits you show and the manner in which you respond.

ABOUT THIS BOOK

This book contains tests divided into Examination Sections. Go through each test, answering every question in the margin. We have also attached a sample answer sheet at the back of the book that can be removed and used. At the end of each test look at the answer key and check your answers. On the ones you got wrong, look at the right answer choice and learn. Do not fill in the answers first. Do not memorize the questions and answers, but understand the answer and principles involved. On your test, the questions will likely be different from the samples. Questions are changed and new ones added. If you understand these past questions you should have success with any changes that arise. Tests may consist of several types of questions. We have additional books on each subject should more study be advisable or necessary for you. Finally, the more you study, the better prepared you will be. This book is intended to be the last thing you study before you walk into the examination room. Prior study of relevant texts is also recommended. NLC publishes some of these in our Fundamental Series. Knowledge and good sense are important factors in passing your exam. Good luck also helps. So now study this Passbook, absorb the material contained within and take that knowledge into the examination. Then do your best to pass that exam.

EXAMINATION SECTION

EXAMINATION SECTION
TEST 1

DIRECTIONS: Each question or incomplete statement is followed by several suggested answers or completions. Select the one that BEST answers the question or completes the statement. *PRINT THE LETTER OF THE CORRECT ANSWER IN THE SPACE AT THE RIGHT.*

1. All of the following are generally accepted moral values basic to clinical nursing practice EXCEPT

    A. nonmaleficence
    B. veracity
    C. countertransference
    D. fidelity

    1.____

2. Values clarification is a process by which individuals find their own answers (values) to situations.
   Valuing is composed of seven processes, that can be placed in which of the following groups?

    A. Prizing one's beliefs and behaviors
    B. Choosing one's beliefs and behaviors
    C. Acting on one's beliefs
    D. All of the above

    2.____

3. Behavior must be consistent over a period of time in order to reflect a value.
   It is important for nurses to do all of the following EXCEPT

    A. examine their own values and clarify them
    B. confront the patient with their values
    C. recognize the differences in the values of peers, other health care professionals, and health care organizations
    D. recognize the differences in the values of patients and accept them

    3.____

4. Which of the following is NOT an advantage of values clarification?

    A. It serves as a guide for assessing patient's values and provides direction for nursing interventions.
    B. It gives insight into the source of a particular value.
    C. It fosters the making of choices.
    D. It sets limits on the type of nursing activities that can be undertaken.

    4.____

5. Values change from time to time as situations change. Reasons for identifying a patient's value system do not include

    A. helping a patient discover a new and meaningful value system following injury or illness
    B. helping the patient explore alternative goals and intervention strategies when valued goals cannot be realized
    C. controlling patient behaviors through value manipulation
    D. planning nursing interventions that support the patient's cultural and health care beliefs

    5.____

6. All of the following are means of learning a patient's values EXCEPT

    6.____

A. conversation with a patient about job, family, pets, hobbies, goals or material possessions
B. trying to adopt an authoritative role in patient's thought process
C. listening to patient's family and friends
D. reviewing patient's health records revealing personal values

7. Different patients exhibit different behaviors. Behaviors that may indicate unclear values include all of the following EXCEPT 7.____

    A. ignoring a health professional's advice
    B. prior history of cooperation and consistent behavior
    C. inconsistent communication or behavior
    D. confusion or uncertainty about which course of action to take

8. An ethical or moral dilemma is a situation involving a choice between equally satisfactory or unsatisfactory alternatives or a difficult problem that seems to have no satisfactory solution. 8.____
    According to Thompson and Thompson, for a situation to be a moral dilemma, it MUST fulfill which of the following criteria?

    A. Awareness of different options
    B. Personal nature of the dilemma
    C. A lack of acceptable alternatives
    D. All of the above

9. Nursing codes of ethics 9.____

    A. provide a means by which professional standards of practice are established, maintained, and improved
    B. give the members of the profession a set of guidelines for negotiating contracts
    C. limit the type of work a nurse can ethically attempt
    D. all of the above

10. Purposes of ethical nursing codes include all of the following EXCEPT 10.____

    A. providing a basis for regulating the relationship between the nurse, patient, coworker, society, and the profession
    B. serving as a basis for professional curricula and for orienting the new graduate to professional nursing practice
    C. providing a standard basis for including the unscrupulous nursing practitioner and for defending a practitioner who is correctly accused
    D. assisting the public in understanding professional nursing conduct

11. All of the following statements agree with the American Nurses Association Code for nurses EXCEPT: 11.____

    A. The patient's right to privacy is safeguarded by judiciously protecting information of a confidential nature
    B. Nurses do not assume responsibility and accountability for individual nursing judgments and actions
    C. Nurses maintain competence in nursing care
    D. Nurses participate in the profession's efforts to implement and improve standards of nursing

12. In addressing the issue of risk versus responsibility to patients, the American Nurses Association presents fundamental criteria to differentiate the nurse's moral duty from the moral option to care for a patient, namely whether

    A. the patient is at significant risk of harm, loss or damage if the nurse does not assist
    B. the nurse's intervention or care is directly relevant to preventing harm
    C. the benefit the patient will gain outweighs any harm the nurse might incur and does not present more than minimal risks to the health care provider
    D. all of the above

13. All of the following statements about the Canadian Nurses Association Code of Ethics for nursing are correct EXCEPT the nurse

    A. is not obliged to hold confidential all information regarding a patient learned in the health care setting
    B. has an obligation to be guided by consideration for the dignity of patients
    C. is obligated to provide competent care to patients
    D. is obligated to represent the ethics of nursing before colleagues and others

14. The withdrawal of equipment from a patient whose life is being sustained by artificial means is a highly complex issue.
    The Hastings Center has prepared guidelines for the termination of life-sustaining treatment, which are governed by all of the following values EXCEPT

    A. the patient's well-being
    B. the nurse's autonomy
    C. integrity of the health professional
    D. justice or equity

15. Although codes of ethics offer general guidelines for decision-making, more specific guidelines are necessary in many cases to resolve the ethical dilemmas encountered by nurses in practice settings.
    Suggested guidelines for nurses to resolve these dilemmas include

    A. establishing a sound data base
    B. disregarding any conflicts presented by the situation
    C. establishing a single course of action in advance
    D. all of the above

16. Nurses need to gather as much information as possible about a situation.
    Aroskar suggests that nurses get answers to all of the following EXCEPT what

    A. persons are involved and what is their involvement in the situation
    B. diagnostic workup the nurse has to perform for a particular case
    C. is the proposed action and what is the intention of the proposed action
    D. are the possible consequences of the proposed action

17. Nursing practice is governed by many legal concepts. Knowledge of laws that regulate and affect nursing practice are needed to
    I. ensure that the nurse's decisions and actions are consistent with current legal principles
    II. protect the nurse from liability
    III. protect the patient
    IV. protect the hospital

The CORRECT answer is:

D. I only   E. II, III   F. I, II   G. I, III, IV

18. Functions of law in nursing do NOT include
    A. providing a framework for establishing which nursing actions in the care of patients are legal
    B. differentiating the nurse's responsibilities from those of the other health professionals
    C. protecting nurses from culpability for their errors
    D. all of the above

19. The Constitutions of the United States and Canada include due process and equal protection clauses. The due process clause applies to state or provincial and local agencies, including public hospitals, and to actions that deprive a person of life, liberty or property. This includes which of the following primary elements?
    A. The rules being applied must be reasonable.
    B. Fair procedures must be followed when enforcing the rules.
    C. The rules being applied must not be vague.
    D. All of the above

20. Laws govern the relationships of private individuals with the government and with each other.
    All of the following are types of law EXCEPT
    A. contact
    B. tort
    C. contract
    D. constitutional

21. Our system of law rests upon all of the following principles EXCEPT:
    A. Law is based on a concern for justice and fairness
    B. Law is characterized by resistance to change
    C. Actions are judged on the basis of a universal standard of what a similarly educated, reasonable and prudent person would have done under similar circumstances
    D. Each individual has rights and responsibilities

22. Licenses are legal permits granted by a government agency for the practice of a profession and the use of a particular title.
    In order for a profession or occupation to need or hold a license, its members must GENERALLY meet which of the following criteria?
    A. There is little need to protect the public's safety or welfare.
    B. The occupation is clearly delineated as a separate and distinct area of work.
    C. There is no organization suitable in ability to assume the obligations of the licensing process.
    D. All of the above

23. The ANA has enumerated the principles of credentialing. These principles reflect the belief that credentialing exists PRIMARILY to protect and benefit the public and includes

    A. accountability as an essential component of any credentialing process
    B. professional identity and responsibility evolving from the credentialing process
    C. an effective system of role delineation
    D. all of the above

24. In the United States, nurses are issued a license by the State Board of Nursing or by an administrative governmental agency.
    Licenses are issued to all of the following registered nurses EXCEPT nurses who have

    A. successfully completed a course of study in a school of nursing accredited by State Board
    B. completed three years of basic training in a private or government hospital
    C. passed the National Qualifying Examinations with a score that is acceptable to the Board
    D. paid the required fees

25. There are two types of licensure/registration: mandatory and permissive.
    Under mandatory licensure, all nursing practice must be licensed EXCEPT practice

    A. in an emergency
    B. by nursing students as part of their education
    C. by nurses employed by the federal government
    D. all of the above

KEY (CORRECT ANSWERS)

1.	C	11.	B
2.	D	12.	D
3.	B	13.	A
4.	D	14.	B
5.	C	15.	A
6.	B	16.	B
7.	B	17.	C
8.	A	18.	C
9.	A	19.	D
10.	C	20.	A

21. B
22. B
23. D
24. B
25. D

TEST 2

DIRECTIONS: Each question or incomplete statement is followed by several suggested answers or completions. Select the one that BEST answers the question or completes the statement. *PRINT THE LETTER OF THE CORRECT ANSWER IN THE SPACE AT THE RIGHT.*

1. A contract is an agreement between two or more competent persons, upon sufficient consideration, to do or not to do some lawful act.
Contract law requires all of the following elements be met in order to make a contract valid EXCEPT

    A. the act contracted for must be legal
    B. there must be no compensation for the service to be provided
    C. there must be mutual agreement about the services to be contracted for
    D. the parties to be contracted must be of legal age and competent to enter a binding agreement

    1.____

2. Nurses have three separate, interdependent legal roles, each with its own rights and associated responsibilities. These roles include

    A. provider of service
    B. employee or contractor for service
    C. citizen
    D. all of the above

    2.____

3. While working in the capacity of employee or contractor for service, a nurse has all of the following legal rights EXCEPT the right to

    A. adequate and qualified assistance as necessary
    B. adequate working conditions, e.g., safe equipment and facilities
    C. compensation for services rendered
    D. reasonable and prudent conduct by other health care givers

    3.____

4. Most jurisdictions of the country have statutes that impose a duty to report certain confidential information. Major reporting categories include all of the following EXCEPT

    A. vital statistics, e.g., births and deaths
    B. infections and communicable diseases
    C. cancer and other serious conditions
    D. child or elder abuse

    4.____

5. A tort is a civil wrong committed against a person or a person's property.
All of the following statements are unintentional torts EXCEPT

    A. they can result from either an act of commission or an act of omission
    B. the act in question is willful and deliberate
    C. the wrong results from failure to use due care
    D. they are not spelled out in an all-inclusive list

    5.____

6. Obtaining informed consent is the responsibility of a physician.
The nurse's responsibility is often to witness the giving of informed consent and involves

    6.____

A. witnessing the exchange between the patient and the physician
B. notarizing the patient's signature
C. determining that the patient really did understand
D. all of the above

7. Northrop describes major elements of informed consent as including all of the following EXCEPT that

   A. the consent must be given voluntarily
   B. the consent must be given by an individual with the capacity and competence to understand
   C. in order to give consent, the patient must feel coerced
   D. the patient must be given enough information to be the ultimate decision maker

7.____

8. The American Heart Association has issued standards and guidelines for cardiopulmonary resuscitation and emergency cardiac care, outlining the medicolegal considerations and offering recommendations about DNR orders for physicians. The implications of the American Heart Association code standards means that a nurse must do all of the following EXCEPT

   A. ensure that the DNR order is written on the patient's order sheet and progress notes
   B. if the physician refuses to write a DNR order, follow agency policies and procedures
   C. even if the agency does not have a well-established procedure, do not seek a legal opinion
   D. if none of the above steps provide the nurse with sufficient guidelines, the nurse must make a personal decision based on moral values and sense of humanity

8.____

9. Clinical guidelines for the legal precautions that a nurse should adopt include

   A. observe and monitor the patient accurately
   B. build and maintain good rapport with patients
   C. protect patients from falls and preventable injuries
   D. all of the above

9.____

10. Abortion laws provide specific guidelines for nurses about what is legally permissible. The results of Supreme Court rulings do NOT include which of the following statements?

    A. It is not legally permissible for the state to restrict or regulate abortions during the first trimester of pregnancy, except to require that abortions be performed by licensed physicians.
    B. During the second trimester of pregnancy, the mother's privacy rights override any restrictions designed to protect the health and safety of the mother.
    C. During the third trimester of pregnancy, the state has the right to prohibit abortion.
    D. All of the above

10.____

11. Nurses are expected to know basic information about procedures and medications ordered by a physician. Becker outlines all of the following orders that nurses must question in order to protect themselves legally EXCEPT to question

11.____

A. any order a patient questions
B. standing orders, especially if the nurse is inexperienced
C. verbal orders to avoid miscommunication
D. any order if the patient's condition remains the same

12. Nursing students are responsible for their actions and are liable for their acts of negligence committed during the course of clinical experience.
In order to fulfill their responsibilities to patients and to minimize chances for liability, nursing students need to do all of the following EXCEPT

   A. make sure they are prepared to carry out the necessary care for assigned patients
   B. not ask for additional help or supervision
   C. comply with the policies of the agency in which they obtain their clinical experience
   D. comply with the policies and definitions of responsibility supplied by the school of nursing

13. A will is a declaration by a person about how the person's property is to be disposed of after death.
In order for a will to be valid, which of the following conditions must be met?

   A. The person making the will must be of sound mind.
   B. The person must not be influenced in any way by anyone else.
   C. The person must be physically healthy.
   D. All of the above

14. In the past, health care facilities have been influenced largely by the needs of the people providing the services. As a result, preventive health care facilities have been slow to develop.
This delay can be attributed in great part to the fact that

   A. physicians are largely oriented toward preventing illness in their practice
   B. consumers have been less aware of treatment of illness then of prevention and health promotion
   C. the nurse's role as the chief provider of preventive health care and health promotion has been slow to evolve
   D. all of the above

15. The health delivery system is very much affected by a country's total economic status.
Correct statements about economic influences include all of the following EXCEPT:

   A. Inflation and the economic recession of the early 1980's brought increasing concern about escalating health care costs
   B. Medical care costs have increased more than 400% since 1965
   C. The United States spends $1 billion a day on health care and costs are still rising
   D. The United States spends more on health care than it does on defense

16. Funding for personal health care can come from a variety of sources.
Major sources include all of the following EXCEPT

   A. governments (social insurance)
   B. individual clients
   C. private organizations
   D. health insurance

17. Primary care agencies are the point of entry into the health care system and the point at which initial health care is given.
    The major purpose of primary care centers is to provide all of the following EXCEPT

    A. long term and chronic care
    B. treatment of permanent malfunctioning that does not require hospitalization
    C. emergency care
    D. health maintenance

    17.____

18. Ambulatory care centers are being used more frequently in many communities. These centers have all of the following advantages EXCEPT they

    A. permit patients to live in a controlled environment while obtaining needed health care
    B. provide medical, nursing, laboratory, and radiologic services
    C. free costly hospital beds for seriously ill patients
    D. all of the above

    18.____

19. An HMO is a group health care agency that provides basic and supplemental health maintenance and treatment services to voluntary enrollees.
    To be federally qualified, an HMO company must meet certain requirements which include offering all of the following EXCEPT

    A. physician's services
    B. short-term mental health services
    C. preventive dental services for children over 12 years of age
    D. laboratory and radiological services

    19.____

20. The preferred provider organization (PPO) has emerged as another alternative health delivery system.
    Major sponsors of PPOs include all of the following EXCEPT

    A. individual patients   B. hospitals
    C. physicians   D. insurance companies

    20.____

21. In 1987, the Congress of the United States passed the Omnibus Budget Reconciliation Act (OBRA) to bring a measure of quality assurance to the nursing home industry. One of the provisions of OBRA that concerns nursing is the requirement for nursing aide training.
    Specific requirements include

    A. a training program of 50 hours for nurse's aides
    B. a registry for nurse's aides
    C. a training program of 25 hours for nurse's aides already providing care
    D. all of the above

    21.____

22. Nursing implications of this 1987 OBRA provision include

    A. concerns about which state agency is to be responsible for implementing the requirements
    B. that the training requirements may not be sufficient to prepare aides to carry out routine care for nursing home patients who have complex problems
    C. the evaluation requirement necessitates job analysis and the development of standard criteria at the state level
    D. all of the above

    22.____

23. The American Hospital Association published *A Patient's Bill of Rights* in an effort to promote the rights of hospitalized clients.
The nursing implications of the patient's bill of rights are that the patient has the right to

   A. considerate and respectful care
   B. refuse treatment to the extent permitted by law
   C. expect reasonable continuity of care
   D. all of the above

23._____

24. The problem of financing health illness services is increasingly severe.
Major reasons for increased costs include all of the following EXCEPT

   A. existing equipment and facilities are continually becoming obsolete as research discovers new and better methods
   B. the relative number of people who provide health illness services has decreased
   C. the total population has grown and the demands for services has increased
   D. inflation increases all costs

24._____

25. The number of homeless people in towns and cities continues to grow.
Reasons for this increase include all of the following EXCEPT

   A. an increase in federal subsidies for low-income housing
   B. alcohol and drug abuse
   C. deinstitutionalization of mental health facilities and a change in laws governing commitment of the mentally ill
   D. the rising cost of housing

25._____

KEY (CORRECT ANSWERS)

1.	B	11.	D
2.	D	12.	B
3.	A	13.	A
4.	C	14.	C
5.	B	15.	D
6.	A	16.	C
7.	C	17.	B
8.	C	18.	A
9.	D	19.	C
10.	B	20.	A

21.	B
22.	D
23.	D
24.	B
25.	A

EXAMINATION SECTION
TEST 1

DIRECTIONS: Each question or incomplete statement is followed by several suggested answers or completions. Select the one that BEST answers the question or completes the statement. *PRINT THE LETTER OF THE CORRECT ANSWER IN THE SPACE AT THE RIGHT.*

1. When problems in communication have been identified, the nurse and client can set goals and begin planning ways to promote effective communication.
   Specific nursing interventions do NOT include

   A. developing listening skills
   B. becoming aware of how people respond
   C. establishing a formal tone
   D. all of the above

   1.____

2. Resistance to change is not merely lack of acceptance but behavior intended to maintain the status quo and to prevent change.
   According to New and Couillard, people resist change for all of the following reasons EXCEPT

   A. threatened self-interest
   B. inaccurate perceptions
   C. objective disagreement with the change
   D. high level of adaptability

   2.____

3. Stevens described different stages of resistance to change, including all of the following EXCEPT

   A. undifferentiated resistance arises from one source
   B. the sides for and against the change line up and develop their stands
   C. the people for the change are in power
   D. the people against the change begin the stages of acceptance

   3.____

4. Reinhard offers all of the following guidelines for dealing with resistance EXCEPT:

   A. Communicate with the people who oppose the change and identify the cause of their opposition
   B. Clarify information and give accurate feedback
   C. Decrease psychological security and reduce threat to it
   D. Maintain a climate of trust, support, and confidence

   4.____

5. Motivation relates to whether the client wants to learn and is usually greatest when the client is ready, the learning need is recognized, and the content is meaningful to the client.
   Nurses can positively influence a client's motivation by

   A. relating the learning to something the client values and helping the client see the relevance of the learning
   B. helping the client to make the learning situation pleasant
   C. encouraging self-direction
   D. all of the above

   5.____

6. Written and verbal communication between health team members is vital to the quality of health care. Accurate complete communication serves several purposes, which include all of the following EXCEPT

   A. helps coordinate care given by several people
   B. prevents the client from having to repeat information to each health team member
   C. presumes accuracy in the provision of care and increases the possibility of error
   D. helps health personnel make the best use of their time by avoiding overlapping of activities

7. In a problem oriented medical record, data about the client is recorded and arranged according to the problems the client has rather than according to the source of information. Its basic components include all of the following EXCEPT

   A. defined database
   B. initial list of orders or care plans
   C. progress notes
   D. physician's order sheet

8. Specific ways in which an automated client care plan can facilitate the role of the nurse includes

   A. entry of nursing assessments is highly complex
   B. system facilitates complete and legible medication orders
   C. use of nursing diagnosis is exacerbated, multiple formats are utilized
   D. all of the above

9. Nursing care rounds are procedures in which a group of nurses visit all or selected patients at their bedside in order to obtain all of the following EXCEPT

   A. information that will help plan nursing care
   B. information about ambulatory care services
   C. an opportunity for patients to discuss their care
   D. an evaluation of the nursing care the patient has received

10. Not all data that a nurse obtains about a client can be recorded. The following guide may assist nurses in selecting essential and complete information to record about clients, including any

    A. behavior changes
    B. retention of physical function
    C. statements made to the patient
    D. all of the above

11. Nursing diagnosis is advocated for all of the following reasons EXCEPT to

    A. aid in identifying and describing the domain and scope of nursing practice
    B. help the doctor in planning for rehabilitation care
    C. prescribe the contents of nursing curricula
    D. lead to more comprehensive and individualized patient care

12. To facilitate the implementation of nursing care plans, appropriate procedures and policies need to be established within the department of nursing itself.
    These should be concerned with matters including questions concerning

    A. who has the responsibility for initiating a nursing care plan
    B. how new staff members are to be oriented
    C. what forms are to be used and where they shall be kept
    D. all of the above

13. Another step in identifying specific program needs is to determine what the cost will be. Factors to consider in determining the cost of an educational program include all of the following EXCEPT

    A. audiovisuals needed, e.g., movies, filmstrips, charts
    B. orthopaedic workshop budget
    C. duplicating costs, e.g., patient information booklets, pamphlets
    D. possible involvement of other departments

14. Nursing department staff will need information sessions so that they can actively support those staff members who are teaching.
    Included in the in-service sessions for the teaching staff should be all of the following EXCEPT

    A. modes of psychoanalysis
    B. purpose of the patient education program
    C. objectives and contents
    D. methods of conveying the content

15. Discharge planning is dependent upon

    A. unexpected outcomes of care
    B. freedom from complications
    C. the availability of resources
    D. all of the above

16. The leadership style adopted by the manager depends a great deal upon all of the following factors EXCEPT the

    A. importance of results
    B. characteristics of workers
    C. personal characteristics of the manager
    D. resources available

17. Strategies that could help a newly appointed chief nursing officer include all of the following EXCEPT

    A. deciding on objectives and sharing them symbolically
    B. developing positive coalitions quickly
    C. minimizing the use of personal charisma to reach your constituents and not relying on it
    D. knowing the institutional legacy

18. The purpose of control is to see that actual performance corresponds to that which is called for in various plans. All effective managers exercise control by

    A. knowing or establishing the standards that relate to a particular course of action
    B. demanding consistent performance above the established standards
    C. punishing all deviations from the standards
    D. all of the above

19. The mutually supportive relationship between the CEO and the CNO can be enhanced by following which of the following practical suggestions?

    A. Detect potential problems and delegate their resolution to subordinate staff
    B. Disregard your visibility
    C. Foster and maintain a positive and active relationship with the medical staff
    D. All of the above

20. Among the influence strategies that effectively channel the elements of the leader's power into productive results are all of the following EXCEPT

    A. obtaining and sharing accurate information
    B. discouraging subordinates from identifying with the leader
    C. using rewards and punishments effectively
    D. understanding how to manipulate cues affecting a decision

21. The different phases of the planning process are interdependent and continuous; they frequently overlap in time and often are not discrete.
    Viewed in phases, the planning process consists of

    A. seeking common purposes and objectives
    B. identifying issues and concerns
    C. determining an organizational structure for planning
    D. all of the above

22. To design and create a planning mechanism adapted to your department's conditions and needs, you must do all of the following EXCEPT

    A. pinpoint data and information needs and availability
    B. avoid setting a tentative timetable
    C. estimate budgetary requirements
    D. identify leaders and select participants for functional tasks

23. The use of data from existing sources presents few problems and precludes elaborate, time-consuming data collection.
    Use of this data involves

    A. identifying their sources
    B. presuming their relevance, timeliness, and accuracy
    C. analyzing the meaning and implications of the data in terms of personal liability
    D. all of the above

24. It is difficult to anticipate the kinds of special studies that may have to be undertaken for a specific planning activity.
    Special studies have been conducted in all of the following areas EXCEPT

    A. patient need for services
    B. salaries and fringe benefits
    C. ambulatory care services
    D. processes of recruitment for nursing

24.____

25. Administering a questionnaire, perhaps the most widely used method for original data collection, is the simplest type of data-collecting method.
    Questionnaires are used to elicit data on all of the following EXCEPT

    A. objective facts
    C. behavioral variables
    B. subjective facts
    D. specified events

25.____

KEY (CORRECT ANSWERS)

1.	C	11.	B
2.	D	12.	D
3.	A	13.	B
4.	C	14.	A
5.	D	15.	C
6.	C	16.	D
7.	D	17.	C
8.	B	18.	A
9.	B	19.	C
10.	A	20.	B

21. D
22. B
23. A
24. C
25. B

TEST 2

DIRECTIONS: Each question or incomplete statement is followed by several suggested answers or completions. Select the one that BEST answers the question or completes the statement. *PRINT THE LETTER OF THE CORRECT ANSWER IN THE SPACE AT THE RIGHT.*

1. When recommendations have been formulated and priorities have been determined, they are then incorporated into a definitive plan for meeting nursing needs.
   In developing the plan, attention is given to

   A. specifying goals, objectives, and policies for carrying out recommendations and suggested programs
   B. indicating the individuals responsible for carrying out each recommendation
   C. specifying a time span for achieving specific objectives or steps in the plan
   D. all of the above

   1.___

2. A plan is good or generally acceptable if it contains all of the following characteristics EXCEPT

   A. is in line with a clearly stated objective
   B. does not allow for alternate courses of action
   C. represents an integrated whole and not an isolated entity
   D. indicates the procedural method for putting the plan into action

   2.___

3. Resisters should become *targets* of the administrator's strategy for making an effective change.
   The administrator should take which of the following steps?

   A. Focus targets' attention on the present, not the future
   B. Assign roles, tasks, and responsibilities to others so target feels pressure to change
   C. Identify anchors who targets can trust and who will remain constant and provide stability
   D. All of the above

   3.___

4. Health system engineers are employed by hospitals and other health care institutions to study facility design and utilization, information flow, and personnel utilization.
   Activities summarizing the services provided by system engineers include

   A. analysis, design, and improvement of work systems, centers, and methods
   B. simplification of paperwork and the design of forms
   C. improvement of organizational structure, authority-responsibility relationships, and patterns of communication
   D. all of the above

   4.___

5. A system is defined as a network of interrelated operations joined together to perform an activity.
   An effective system should produce all of the following important results EXCEPT

   A. the right information furnished to the right people at the right time, and at the right cost
   B. a decrease in uncertainty and improvement of decision quality
   C. a decreased capacity to process the present and future volume of work
   D. an ability to perform profitable work that was previously impossible

   5.___

6. Styles writes that nursing organizations must perform functions for the preservation and development of the profession, including   6.____

   A. professional definition and regulation through the setting and enforcing of standards of education and practice for the generalist and specialist
   B. development of the knowledge base for practice in only broadest components
   C. defining the legal ramifications of nursing standards and limiting liability at all costs
   D. all of the above

7. The ANA Commission on Nursing Research identifies all of the following as priorities for nursing research EXCEPT   7.____

   A. promoting health and preventing illness
   B. increasing the negative impact of health problems on coping abilities, productivity, and satisfaction
   C. developing strategies that provide effective nursing care to high-risk and vulnerable groups
   D. developing cost-efficient delivery systems of nursing care

8. Nursing involves an interrelationship between many people concerned with a client's responses to potential or actual health problems.
   Nursing practice involves four areas related to health, including all of the following EXCEPT   8.____

   A. health promotion   B. ambulatory care
   C. health restoration   D. care of the dying

9. Although all graduate schools have somewhat different requirements, common requirements for admission to graduate programs in nursing do NOT include that the applicant must   9.____

   A. be a registered nurse
   B. give evidence of scholastic ability
   C. score in the top 20% on a qualifying examination
   D. all of the above

10. The term *continuing education* refers to formalized experiences designed to enlarge the knowledge or skills of practitioners.
    Continuing education is usually designed to   10.____

    A. keep nurses abreast of new techniques and knowledge
    B. help nurses through enhancing their research skills
    C. provide nurses with information essential to avoid legal liability
    D. all of the above

11. Socialization can be defined as the process by which people learn to become members of society.
    All of the following are characteristics of socialization EXCEPT it   11.____

    A. is a reciprocal learning process brought about by interaction with other people
    B. does not establish boundaries of behavior
    C. develops a social self or awareness of others and their expectations
    D. is basic to group continuity and stability

12. Professional or occupational socialization is a very important part of adult socialization. The professional education concept of the nurse is one who

    A. defines clients in terms of their economic potential
    B. views the relationship between the nurse and client as a therapeutic and analytic process
    C. accepts legal responsibility and accountability for client health and welfare
    D. all of the above

13. It is within the nursing education program that professional values are developed, clarified, and internalized. Watson outlined values critical for the profession of nursing, which include all of the following EXCEPT

    A. a strong commitment to the service that nursing provides for the public
    B. belief in the dignity and worth of each person
    C. autonomy
    D. professional socialization

14. Several models have been developed to explain the initial process of socialization into professional roles.
    Ida Harper Simpson outlined three distinct phases of professional socialization, which include all of the following EXCEPT

    A. psyching out and role stimulation
    B. person concentrates on becoming proficient in specific work tasks
    C. person becomes attached to significant others in the work or reference group
    D. person internalizes the values of the professional group and adopts the prescribed behaviors

15. Hinshaw provided a three-phase general model of socialization that was an adaptation of Simpson's model.
    This model includes all of the following EXCEPT

    A. transition of anticipatory role expectations to role expectations of a societal group
    B. attachment to significant other/label incongruencies
    C. initial innocence
    D. internalization of role values

16. An advocate pleads the cause of another or argues or pleads for a cause or proposal. Underlying client advocacy is the belief that individuals have the right to

    A. select values they deem necessary to sustain their lives
    B. exercise judgment of the best course of action to achieve the chosen value
    C. dispose of values in a way they choose without coercion by others
    D. all of the above

17. A change agent is a person or group who initiates changes or who assists others in making modifications in themselves or in the system.
    Lancaster and Lancaster describe the function of a change agent in assisting a group as

A. determining if a problem exists
B. deciding on the appropriate course of action
C. helping to develop an evaluation format
D. all of the above

18. Nursing leadership is defined as the process of interpersonal influences through which a client is assisted in the establishment and achievement of goals towards improved well-being.
The purposes of leadership vary according to the level of application and include all of the following EXCEPT

    A. improving the health status of individuals or families
    B. increasing the effectiveness and level of satisfaction among professional colleagues who provide care
    C. improving the attitudes of citizens and legislators toward the nursing profession and their expectations of it
    D. providing increasing home care services

19. Participative leadership is an approach to group leadership in which functions are distributed. Participative leaders are guided by the principles that

    A. leadership is concentrated in one primary member of the group
    B. formal or designated leadership is unconditional and other members may not perform functions equal in importance to or more important than those of the formal leader
    C. leadership is a set of learned behaviors
    D. all of the above

20. Many constraints in clinical settings must be reckoned with before research can become a legitimate and comfortable activity.
However, if nursing is to develop as a research-based practice, it is NOT unreasonable to expect the nurse in the clinical area to demonstrate

    A. complete awareness of the process and language of research
    B. sensitivity to issues related to protecting the rights of human subjects
    C. an indiscriminate consumption of research findings
    D. all of the above

21. Change is the process which leads to alteration in individual or institutional patterns of behavior. A nurse can use a number of strategies to implement change.
The three categories described by Bennis, Benne, and Chin do NOT include

    A. power-coercive   B. empiric-rational
    C. situational-demonstrative   D. all of the above

22. Nursing research is more than scientific investigation conducted by a person educated and credentialed as a nurse.
Diers enumerated three distinguishing properties of nursing research which states that

    A. the final focus of nursing research must be on a difference that matters in improving client care

B. nursing research has the potential for contributing to individual patient care
C. a research problem is a nursing research problem when nurses do not have access to or control over the phenomena being studied
D. all of the above

23. Automated client care systems allow *on-line* use of standardized nursing care plans. A specific way in which an automated client care plan can facilitate the role of the nurse does not include that

    A. laboratory data can be ordered by entering a request at a computer workstation
    B. the system cannot facilitate complete medications orders
    C. the system promotes consistent doctors' orders
    D. the use of nursing diagnosis is facilitated because a common format can be used

24. Theory development is considered by many nurses to be one of the most crucial tasks facing the profession today. Three approaches may be used to develop nursing theory including

    A. borrowing conceptual framework from other disciplines and applying them to nursing problems
    B. using a reductive approach
    C. using a subjective approach
    D. all of the above

25. The beliefs underlying a profession are its value system. Generally, these beliefs are similar from model to model and state that

    A. nurses have a unique function even though they share certain functions with other health professionals
    B. nursing uses a systematic process to operationalize its conceptual model
    C. nursing involves a series of interpersonal relationships
    D. all of the above

KEY (CORRECT ANSWERS)

1. D
2. B
3. C
4. D
5. C

6. A
7. B
8. B
9. C
10. A

11. B
12. B
13. D
14. A
15. C

16. D
17. C
18. D
19. C
20. B

21. C
22. A
23. B
24. A
25. D

EXAMINATION SECTION
TEST 1

DIRECTIONS: Each question or incomplete statement is followed by several suggested answers or completions. Select the one that BEST answers the question or completes the statement. *PRINT THE LETTER OF THE CORRECT ANSWER IN THE SPACE AT THE RIGHT.*

1. Which of the following is NOT a goal associated with the use of critical pathways in medical care.
   To

   A. promote professional and collaborative practice and care
   B. establish standards of practice for health care professionals
   C. achieve realistic, expected client and family outcomes
   D. reduce costs and the length of stay

2. The organization largely responsible for the voluntary accreditation of nursing education programs in the United States is the

   A. National League for Nursing (NLN)
   B. International Council of Nurses (ICN)
   C. Joint Commission on Accreditation of Healthcare Organizations (JCAHO)
   D. American Nurses Association (ANA)

3. Which of the following is NOT generally considered to be a goal of the contemporary health care system?

   A. Return of autonomy and independence to the client
   B. Return of health care professionals to more generalized education and practice
   C. Increased emphasis on preventive care
   D. Acceptance of good health as a responsibility of the client, care provider, and society

4. Nurses who want to ensure their autonomy in the workplace generally seek

   A. administrative positions
   B. research positions
   C. expanded clinical competence
   D. private practice

5. Each of the following was a feature of Florence Nightingale's original nursing program at St. Thomas Hospital EXCEPT that

   A. the program was financially linked to the hospital
   B. the training lasted 1 year
   C. records were kept on student and graduate progress for the purpose of establishing standards
   D. training included both formal instruction and practical experience

6. The earliest mode of nursing care in use was

   A. team nursing
   B. the case method
   C. the functional method
   D. primary nursing

7. The body of law that defines and enforces duties and rights among private individuals that are not based on contractual agreements is _____ law.

   A. criminal   B. private   C. tort   D. public

8. According to Miller, the degree to which a nurse functions as a professional is reflected in each of the following behaviors EXCEPT

   A. assessing, planning, implementing, and evaluating theory
   B. preserving and promoting the professional organization as the major referent
   C. accepting, promoting, and maintaining the independence of nursing research from nursing practice
   D. upholding the service orientation of nursing in the public eye

9. If a nurse is inequitably assigned to a shift or weekend work, the category of collective bargaining that has been breached is

   A. violations of federal or state law
   B. contract violations
   C. management responsibilities
   D. violation of agency rules

10. Immediately after World War II, the United States experienced a dire shortage of civilian nurses. The primary reason for this was

    A. a lack of clear nursing education standards for nursing education and practice
    B. low pay and poor working conditions for civilian nurses as opposed to nurses in military service
    C. growth and diversity became a major emphasis in the health care industry
    D. a marked increase in the civilian population

11. In the United States, the system of law rests on four basic principles. Which of the following is NOT one of these?

    A. Each individual has rights and responsibilities.
    B. Law is characterized by change.
    C. Law is based on a concern for the distribution of material wealth and the opportunity to acquire it.
    D. Actions are judged on the basis of a universal standard of what a similarly educated, reasonable, and prudent person would have done under similar circumstances.

12. As a general rule, professional codes of ethics are

    A. typically more demanding than legal standards
    B. used as a framework for legislation
    C. composed in order to protect members of the profession from legal action
    D. formulated in order to conform to legal standards

13. The _____ approach to nursing research is also known as the literary or critical approach.

    A. nonexperimental   B. experimental
    C. qualitative   D. historical

14. Which of the following promoted the facilitation of the *body's reparative processes* by manipulating a patient's environment?   14.____

    A. Rogers
    B. Maslow
    C. Levine
    D. Nightingale

15. If a nurse makes a documentation error while charting a patient, the nurse should _____, write *error in charting* above the incorrect section, and initial the changes.   15.____

    A. cross out the error with a single line
    B. *white out* the error
    C. in a differently colored ink, draw an enclosure around the error
    D. skip a line

16. The ANA recommends that each of the following questions be part of the nursing admission assessment regarding advanced directives EXCEPT: 16.____

    A. Is the client preparing for a procedure for which an advance care directive might be applicable?
    B. Does the client wish to initiate an advance care directive?
    C. Does the client have basic information about advanced directives?
    D. If the client has prepared an advance care directive, did the client bring it to the health care agency?

17. The amount of autonomy a professional group possesses depends *primarily* on its effectiveness at   17.____

    A. governing its members
    B. delineating a professional code of ethics
    C. securing rights for its members
    D. providing legal protection for its members

18. The hospice movement in the United States gathered most of its momentum in the   18.____

    A. 1950s   B. 1960s   C. 1970s   D. 1980s

19. Analysis is a feature of the _____ phase of the nursing process.   19.____

    A. planning
    B. assessing
    C. diagnosing
    D. evaluating

20. When documenting care and observations in a patient record,   20.____

    A. approved medical terms and abbreviations can be used
    B. black or dark blue ink should be used
    C. abbreviation should be avoided at all times to avoid errors
    D. locally adopted abbreviations can be used

21. Which of the following is LEAST likely to factor in nurses' ethical decision-making?   21.____

    A. The professional code ethics
    B. Moral principles
    C. Legal principles
    D. Nurses' perception of roles and responsibilities

22. In order to protect themselves legally, nurses must question each of the following types of orders from physicians EXCEPT

    A. those that differ in any way from those conventionally encountered in similar situations
    B. those given after a client's condition has changed
    C. those that a client questions
    D. standing orders

23. The professional organization for nurses in the United States is the

    A. International Council of Nurses (ICN)
    B. American Nursing Association (ANA)
    C. National Federation of Licensed Practical Nurses (NFLPN)
    D. National League for Nursing (NLN)

24. Which of the following is an example of a secondary health care service?

    A. Preventive care
    B. Advanced specialized diagnostic care
    C. Referral to specialists
    D. Surgery

25. Today, the most significant effect of advances in technology and knowledge in the health care industry has been to

    A. improve diagnostic procedures
    B. change the profile of the hospital client
    C. increase the specialization of professionals
    D. make more effective drugs available to clients

KEY (CORRECT ANSWERS)

1. B		11. C	
2. A		12. A	
3. B		13. D	
4. A		14. D	
5. A		15. A	
6. B		16. A	
7. C		17. A	
8. C		18. C	
9. B		19. C	
10. B		20. A	

21. C
22. A
23. B
24. D
25. B

TEST 2

DIRECTIONS: Each question or incomplete statement is followed by several suggested answers or completions. Select the one that BEST answers the question or completes the statement. *PRINT THE LETTER OF THE CORRECT ANSWER IN TEE SPACE AT THE RIGHT.*

1. Each of the following is a category used to define different clinical specialties for nursing EXCEPT 1.____

    A. illnesses
    B. age groups
    C. locales
    D. teaching

2. In 1945, 2.____

    A. the National League for Nursing established a Department of Practical Nursing
    B. New York became the only state to have mandatory licensure laws for practical nurses
    C. the Smith-Hughes Act was passed
    D. the association of Practical Nursing Schools was founded

3. A nurse becomes _____ by the process of learning the ways of the nursing culture, and becoming a functioning participant in this group. 3.____

    A. proficient
    B. socialized
    C. autonomous
    D. professional

4. Each of the following is a burden of proof required for nursing negligence and malpractice EXCEPT a(n) 4.____

    A. injury to the client
    B. duty of the nurse to the client
    C. causal relationship between the nurse's breach of duty and the subsequent injury to the client
    D. willful breach of the nurse's duty to the client

5. Which of the following is a typical research function of a nurse at the baccalaureate level? 5.____

    A. Assisting others to apply scientific knowledge in nursing practice
    B. Conducting investigations for the purpose of monitoring the quality of practice of nursing in a clinical setting
    C. Identifying nursing problems that need to be investigated and participates in the implementation of specific studies
    D. Developing methods for scientific inquiry of phenomena relevant to nursing

6. Which of the following is NOT a typical characteristic of an Independent Practice Association (IPA)? 6.____

    A. Clients pay a fixed prospective payment to the IPA.
    B. Care is provided in physicians' offices.
    C. At the end of a fiscal year, any surplus money is divided among the provider and the IPA.
    D. The IPA pays the provider directly.

27

7. Nursing _____ includes knowledge obtained through nursing research. 7._____

   A. ethics B. science C. theory D. esthetics

8. Which of the following is an example of constitutional law affecting nurses? 8._____

   A. Living wills
   B. Nurse and employer contracts
   C. Sexual harassment laws
   D. Due process

9. Of the following, which moral framework is based on relationships, rather than on the concept of justice? 9._____

   A. Teleology   B. The ethic of caring
   C. Intuitionism   D. Bioethics

10. A *novice* is a nurse 10._____

    A. who can demonstrate marginally accepted performance
    B. who enters a clinical setting with no experience
    C. who has not yet begun nursing education
    D. whose practice is essentially flexible

11. Each of the following is a basic rule for a nurse to follow in charting a patient EXCEPT 11._____

    A. mark each block of a charting or entry with one's initials
    B. all sheets should contain the patient name, date, and time
    C. use direct quotes when appropriate
    D. use only black ink

12. In what year had all states passed licensure laws affecting practical/vocational nurse training? 12._____

    A. 1914 B. 1941 C. 1955 D. 1961

13. The main DISADVANTAGE associated with the functional mode of nursing care delivery is 13._____

    A. fragmentation of care
    B. economic inefficiency
    C. high personnel demand
    D. overwhelming emotional involvement with client

14. Which of the following is an example of a major tertiary care provider? 14._____

    A. Long-term care facility
    B. Home health care agency
    C. Industrial clinic
    D. Ambulatory care center

15. Which of the following is a characteristic that most clearly distinguishes a profession from other kinds of occupations? 15._____

A. An orientation of the individual toward service, either to a community or to an organization
B. The interdependence of individuals for the advancement of the occupation's influence on the greater culture
C. A long history of the occupation's development and change over time
D. Its requirement for involvement of practitioners in a society's greater civic culture

16. Each of the following is a reason why preventive health care facilities have been slow to develop in the United States EXCEPT 16.____

    A. consumers have been more aware of treatment of illness than of prevention and health promotion
    B. preventive health costs are not covered by most private insurers
    C. physicians are largely oriented to illness in their practice
    D. the nurse's role as chief provider of preventive health care has been slow to evolve, and the treatment of illness often takes precedence over preventive health care activities

17. When developing a definition of health, one should consider that health is 17.____

    A. a condition of physical, mental, and social well-being and absence of disease
    B. a static condition; the absence of pathology
    C. the ability to pursue the activities of daily living
    D. a function of the physiological state

18. In what year was the Patient Self-Determination Act passed by the United States government? 18.____

    A. 1965   B. 1973   C. 1980   D. 1991

19. Which of the following is NOT a purpose generally served by nursing ethics committees? To 19.____

    A. evaluate institutional experiences related to reviewing decisions having ethical implications
    B. direct educational programs that provide knowledge regarding ethical principles and issues for the medical and professional community
    C. participate in disciplinary actions involving nurses who have proven to be in violation of the agency's code of ethics
    D. assist hospital nursing and medical staff in the development and review of policies related to ethical responsibilities

20. The listing of a nurse's name and other information on an official roster of a governmental or nongovernmental agency is a process known as 20.____

    A. licensing   B. registration
    C. credentialing   D. certification

21. As the nursing process method first came into accepted use, most practitioners' attention was focused on 21.____

    A. diagnosing   B. assessing
    C. evaluating   D. implementing

22. Which of the following states uses a Title Act, rather than a practice act, to regulate nursing licensure?

    A. Florida
    B. Ohio
    C. Texas
    D. California

23. The ANA's Human Rights Guideline for Nurses in Clinical and Other Research attempts to specify each of the following EXCEPT the

    A. type of research activities appropriate for nurses at differing educational levels
    B. type of activities involved
    C. mechanisms necessary to ensure that protection is adequate
    D. persons to be safeguarded

24. In 1973, the

    A. Omnibus Budget Reconciliation Act was passed
    B. Health Maintenance Organization Act was passed
    C. Center for Disease Control was established
    D. National Institutes of Health were founded

25. Which of the following is NOT a type of critical pathway variance?

    A. System   B. Treatment   C. Provider   D. Client

KEY (CORRECT ANSWERS

1. D
2. B
3. B
4. D
5. C

6. C
7. B
8. D
9. B
10. B

11. A
12. C
13. A
14. B
15. A

16. B
17. A
18. D
19. C
20. B

21. B
22. C
23. A
24. B
25. B

TEST 3

DIRECTIONS: Each question or incomplete statement is followed by several suggested answers or completions. Select the one that BEST answers the question or completes the statement. *PRINT THE LETTER OF THE COERECT ANSWER IN THE SPACE AT THE RIGHT.*

Questions 1-12.

DIRECTIONS: Questions 1 through 12 refer to the list below of several theorists and practitioners who have contributed to the development of nursing as a profession. In the space at the right of each person's main theory of nursing, place the letter that corresponds to the person's name.

- A. Levine
- B. King
- C. Rogers
- D. Orem
- E. Orlando
- F. Henderson
- G. Watson
- H. Travelbee
- I. Leininger
- J. Neuman
- K. Abdellah
- L. Parse

1. The three elements of the nursing situation are patient behavior, nurse reaction, and nurse action.   1.____

2. A nurse's goal is to be kind and caring but also intelligent, competent, and technically well-prepared to provide service to individuals, families, and society.   2.____

3. The goal of nursing is to use conservation activities aimed at optimal use of a patient's resources.   3.____

4. Caring is assisting persons in performing activities they would accomplish independently given the necessary resources.   4.____

5. The goal of nursing is to maintain and promote health, prevent illness, and care for and rehabilitate ill and disabled patients through the *humanistic science of nursing*.   5.____

6. The interpersonal process is viewed as a human-to-human relationship formed during an illness or *experience of suffering*.   6.____

7. The focus of nursing is on humanity as a living unity, and its qualitative participation with health experience. Health is a continual, open process, rather than a state of well-being or an absence of disease.   7.____

8. Nursing is defined as a process of action, reaction, and interaction whereby nurse and client share information about their perceptions in the nursing situation, leading to goal attainment.   8.____

9. The goal of nursing is to provide care consistent with nursing's emerging science and knowledge, with care as the central focus.   9.____

10. Nursing's primary concern is persons and their self-care actions.   10.____

11. Stress reduction is the goal of the systems model of nursing.   11.____

12. Caring is an interpersonal process comprising interventions that result in meeting human needs.   12.____

13. In 1965, the American Nurses Association published a position paper outlining its beliefs about the nursing profession. Which of the following was NOT a belief included in this paper?

    A. The minimum preparation for technical nursing practice should be an associate degree in nursing.
    B. Nursing assistants should have preservice programs in vocational education, rather than on-the-job training.
    C. The minimum preparation for the beginning professional nurse should be baccalaureate degree in nursing.
    D. Nursing education should take place in affiliation with a health care institution, typically a general hospital.

14. Those acts that are permitted to be performed or prohibited from being performed by a prudent person working within the parameters of his/her training, license, and experience, and the conditions existing at the time, are defined broadly as

    A. the Code of Ethics
    B. the nurse practice act
    C. Standard Operating Procedures
    D. Standards of Care

15. Documentation is part of the _____ phases of the nursing process.

    A. assessment
    B. planning
    C. implementation
    D. evaluation

16. Nursing's first professional code of ethics was adopted in

    A. 1860   B. 1941   C. 1953   D. 1980

17. Mrs. Yardley is a hospital patient with congestive heart failure. She is a bit forgetful and unsteady on her feet. In the past, she has fallen several times, and the nursing staff is concerned for her safety. After some consideration, Mrs. Yardley is provided with a safety reminder device when the nurse cannot be in attendance. The necessary action for Mrs. Yardley's protection interferes, out of necessity, with her ability or tendency to function independently.
    This situation becomes a potential threat to her

    A. nonmaleficence
    B. value system
    C. autonomy
    D. informed consent

18. The ANA's Patient's Bill of Rights includes each of the following elements EXCEPT

    A. a hospital must ask the client about any advance directive before certain procedures are begun
    B. the client's right to refuse a treatment or particular plan of care
    C. if a client lacks decision-making capacity for any reason, the rights will be exercised on their behalf at the discretion of the physician who is currently treating or caring for the client
    D. confidentiality of all records and communications regarding a client's care

19. A nurse _____ provides bedside or direct care in a specialty area.

    A. practitioner   B. clinician
    C. generalist   D. specialist

20. Which of the following is an example of statutory law affecting nurses?

    A. Nurse practice acts   B. Active euthanasia
    C. Negligence   D. Equal protection

21. Which of the following is NOT a type of primary health care agency?

    A. Industrial clinic   B. Ambulatory care center
    C. Hospital   D. Physician's office

22. A profession is considered to be autonomous if it(s)

    A. standards are legislated by a federal government
    B. regulates itself and sets standards for its members
    C. is divided into a federation of regionally independent factions
    D. members are affiliated with a national organization

23. A nurse, committed to the sanctity of life, wants a client to have artificial nutrition and hydration. However, the nurse also knows that tube-feedings are prolonging the client's pain and suffering, and this makes the nurse want to discontinue the feedings. This is an example of

    A. a decision-focused ethical problem
    B. an action-focused ethical problem
    C. intuitionism
    D. moral distress

24. _____ nursing research approach organizes narrative or words to discover themes and relationships among concepts in a non-numerical way.

    A. Nonexperimental   B. Experimental
    C. Qualitative   D. Historical

25. In what year did Florence Nightingale begin the transformation of nursing from occupation to profession by establishing the nursing school at St. Thomas Hospital in London?

    A. 1853   B. 1860   C. 1873   D. 1894

KEY (CORRECT ANSWERS)

1. E
2. K
3. A
4. F
5. C

6. H
7. L
8. B
9. I
10. D

11. J
12. G
13. D
14. D
15. C

16. C
17. C
18. C
19. B
20. A

21. C
22. B
23. A
24. C
25. B

EXAMINATION SECTION
TEST 1

DIRECTIONS: Each question or incomplete statement is followed by several suggested answers or completions. Select the one that BEST answers the question or completes the statement. *PRINT THE LETTER OF THE CORRECT ANSWER IN THE SPACE AT THE RIGHT.*

1. A nurse has reached a level of professionalism categorized as *proficient* when he or she

    A. consciously and deliberately plans nursing care and coordinates complex care demands
    B. recognizes a client's readiness to learn how to manage a treatment program
    C. no longer relies on rules or guidelines
    D. perceives a situation as a whole, rather than just its individual aspects

2. A nurse's separate but interdependent legal roles are generally defined as each of the following EXCEPT

    A. provider of service
    B. citizen
    C. guardian
    D. employee or contractor for service

3. Administrative law is written within the scope of the authority granted by the

    A. long-term care facility   B. hospital
    C. legislative body   D. school of nursing

4. In 1992, the American Organization of Nursing Executives published its recommendations for effective health care reform in the United States. Which of the following was NOT an element of these recommendations?

    A. Finance health care through an increasing reliance on public-sector funding
    B. Increase health care access by the use of physician and non-physician providers
    C. Make provisions for catastrophic care, with some limitation on extraordinary procedures
    D. Encourage consumer partnerships

5. What is the term for the ongoing process of behaving in ways that lead to improved health, or a subjective perception of balance, harmony, and vitality?

    A. Yin   B. Wellness
    C. Soundness   D. Fitness

6. The *adaptive* model of nursing was developed by

    A. Watson   B. Roy
    C. Parse   D. Nightingale

7. The voluntary practice of establishing that an individual nurse has met his/her minimum standards of nursing competence in specialized areas is known as

    A. licensing   B. registration
    C. credentialing   D. certification

8. According to Peplau, the first phase to develop in a nurse-patient relationship is 8.____

   A. resolution B. identification
   C. orientation D. exploitation

9. The purpose of a nurse's professional code of ethics is, in its most general sense, to 9.____

   A. provide standards of conduct for the practice of nursing
   B. provide a tool for interpretation of individual expectations
   C. clearly govern the practice of nursing
   D. state the specific decision-making steps in an ethical dilemma

10. A rehabilitation process typically has each of the following broad objectives EXCEPT to 10.____

    A. assist the client to use his or her abilities
    B. return affected abilities to the highest possible level of function
    C. strengthen existing abilities in order to compensate for the loss of others
    D. prevent further disability

11. Persons who perform emergency care in a reasonable and prudent manner, without appropriate equipment and supplies, are protected from legal action in most states by 11.____

    A. common law B. Good Samaritan laws
    C. liability insurance D. nursing practice acts

12. The central concept of _____ is improving or maintaining the quality of life, rather than saving life or curing illness. 12.____

    A. the health maintenance organization (HMO)
    B. an independent practice association
    C. hospice services
    D. rehabilitation services

13. The purpose of conscience clauses in state abortion legislation is to 13.____

    A. allow medical professionals to refuse participation in third-trimester abortions only
    B. grant hospitals the right to deny admission to abortion clients
    C. implement the federal *gag rule* in hospitals or counseling services about the mention of abortion as an available option
    D. permit nurses or other medical staff to inform patients of their moral obligation to certain procedures

14. Each of the following is true of intentional torts EXCEPT 14.____

    A. the act in question is willful and deliberate
    B. the wrong results from failure to use due care
    C. they involve the commission of a prohibited act
    D. they involve certain specific types of conduct listed as *wrong*

15. In which of the following states would a nursing program use the term *vocational nursing* instead of *practical nursing*? 15.____

    A. California B. New York
    C. Illinois D. Hawaii

16. Which of the following modes of nursing care was developed in response to the shortage of personnel experienced in World War II?   16.____

    A. Team nursing   B. The case method
    C. The functional method   D. Primary nursing

17. Most jurisdictions in the United States have statutes that impose a duty on health care professionals to report certain confidential information. Which of the following is NOT a type of information generally included in these statutes?   17.____

    A. Vital statistics   B. Child or elder abuse
    C. Requested medication   D. Violent incidents

18. In most states, advanced directives   18.____

    A. must be witnessed by at least one person
    B. must be witnessed by two people but do not require review by attorney
    C. may be challenged by members of the client's family
    D. must under all circumstances be reviewed by an attorney

19. The changing nature of the American health care system has involved many implications for nursing practice. Which of the following is NOT one of these?   19.____

    A. Greater demand for assessment and evaluation skills
    B. Demand for researching the cost of nursing care in relation to DRG categories
    C. Greater ability to adapt to a more corporate structure
    D. Decreased need for nurses to function in primary care

20. Nursing interventions that are based on the instructions or written orders of another professional are classified as   20.____

    A. dependent   B. interdependent
    C. released   D. independent

21. A _____ can, under certain circumstances, provide informed consent.   21.____

    A. minor
    B. person who is unconscious
    C. client who is sedated and disoriented
    D. mentally ill person who has been judged to be incompetent

22. Which of the following organizations receives and manages funds and trusts that contribute to the advancement of nursing?   22.____

    A. International Council of Nurses (ICN)
    B. American Nursing Association (ANA)
    C. National Federation of Licensed Practical Nurses (NFLPN)
    D. National League for Nursing (NLN)

23. Which of the following is NOT an example of a primary health care service?   23.____

    A. Illness prevention programs
    B. Referring clients to specialists
    C. Restoring clients to useful function in some or all areas of their lives
    D. Explaining a client's overall health problem

24. A health care professional's duty to do no harm is known as the principle of   24.____

   A. nonmaleficence
   C. beneficence
   B. autonomy
   D. justice

25. The legal term for touching another's body without consent is   25.____

   A. assault
   C. battery
   B. molestation
   D. malicious wounding

KEY (CORRECT ANSWERS)

1. D
2. C
3. C
4. A
5. B

6. B
7. D
8. C
9. A
10. C

11. B
12. C
13. B
14. B
15. A

16. C
17. C
18. B
19. D
20. A

21. A
22. A
23. C
24. A
25. C

TEST 2

DIRECTIONS: Each question or incomplete statement is followed by several suggested answers or completions. Select the one that BEST answers the question or completes the statement. *PRINT THE LETTER OF THE CORRECT ANSWER IN THE SPACE AT THE RIGHT.*

1. The MAIN difference between a Preferred Provider Organization (PPO) and a Preferred Provider Arrangement (PPA) involves 1.____

   A. prepaid premiums
   B. whether services are offered to the insurer at a discounted rate
   C. the degree to which a copayment is applied to services
   D. whether a contract is made with individual providers or an organization of providers

2. The term for a mental image or classification of things and events in terms of similarities is 2.____

   A. framework   B. concept   C. model   D. theory

3. Which of the following is NOT a type of advanced medical directive? 3.____

   A. Durable power of attorney
   B. Living will
   C. Power of executor
   D. Health care proxy

4. A patient has signed a consent for a perineal surgical procedure. Consent will be most clearly indicated by the patient's statement that 4.____

   A. he understands but does not know exactly what will be done during the procedure
   B. his wife wants him to go through with the procedure
   C. he understands the stoma may be permanent
   D. he is in so much pain, he'll sign anything

5. By the end of the nineteenth century, there were three nursing schools established in the United States. Which of the following was NOT one of these? 5.____

   A. Connecticut Training School
   B. Bellevue Hospital School of Nursing
   C. Johns Hopkins School of Nursing
   D. Boston Training School

6. Nursing _____ is the term for the way in which nursing knowledge is expressed by a practitioner. 6.____

   A. ethics   B. science   C. theory   D. esthetics

7. The time period of a civil litigation procedure is LEAST likely to be affected by 7.____

   A. whether an injury or death is involved
   B. the attorneys for both sides
   C. the severity of the complaint
   D. the backlog of cases pending before the court

8. Which of the following is a characteristic that most clearly distinguishes a profession from other kinds of occupations?

   A. A code of ethics
   B. A complex, sophisticated research apparatus devoted to the enlargement of the body of knowledge pertinent to the role to be performed
   C. The esteem with which members of a society's general population regard the occupation
   D. Its requirement of prolonged specialized training to acquire a body of knowledge pertinent to the role to be performed

9. _____ is covered under Medicare.

   A. Dentures
   B. Examinations to prescribe eyeglasses
   C. Examinations to prescribe and fit hearing aids
   D. Dental care

10. The giving of nursing care is an element of the _____ phase of the nursing process.

    A. implementing   B. assessing
    C. diagnosing   D. evaluating

11. Of the following, the first to offer a definition of *nursing process* was

    A. King   B. Travelbee   C. Abdellah   D. Henderson

12. What type of nursing research has proven to be most difficult to carry out in hospital settings?

    A. Nonexperimental   B. Experimental
    C. Qualitative   D. Historical

13. Each of the following is a general approach to moral theory involved in medical practice EXCEPT

    A. teleology   B. bioethics
    C. intuitionism   D. deontology

14. _____ is a system in which one nurse is responsible for total care of a number of clients 24 hours a day, seven days a week.

    A. Team nursing   B. Case-method
    C. Functional-method   D. Primary nursing

15. The purpose of the prospective payment system (PPS) legislation passed by the federal government in 1983 was *primarily* to

    A. create diagnostic categories for reimbursement
    B. limit the amount of money paid to hospitals that are reimbursed by Medicare
    C. fix the amount of coinsurance for Medicare clients
    D. establish a means of determining reimbursements to providers

16. When performing aggregation, a nurse's FIRST step is to

    A. establish relationships
    B. conduct nursing research

C. collect and summarize clinical interventions
D. develop nursing theory

17. The most common malpractice situations involved in nursing care are 17.____

    A. not giving proper attention to patient complaints
    B. medication errors
    C. client falls
    D. mistaken identity

18. A patient's health records are 18.____

    A. owned by the patient, who always has a right to see them
    B. confidential information that can never be taken to court
    C. concise legal records of all care given and responses
    D. not used by anyone but direct care providers

19. Each of the following is a service or agency that has been added to some hospitals as a result of the changing nature of the health care delivery system EXCEPT 19.____

    A. hospice services   B. nutrition classes
    C. elderly day care   D. fitness classes

20. An LPN is working as a staff member at a nursing home. One of the patients, Mr. Thompson, a 90-year-old, is restless and has spent the last few nights wandering about, unable to sleep. The LPN is told in report by Ms. Barkley, a fellow nurse, that Ms. Barkley borrowed a Darvocet from another patient and gave it to Mr. Thompson to calm him down. After the LPN discusses the problem with Ms. Barkley and reports the error to the physician, the next appropriate action would be to 20.____

    A. call her attorney to file a complaint
    B. bring the issue to the organization's ethics committee
    C. report the problem to the State Department of Health
    D. do nothing, since an oral reprimand was given

21. The regulation of nursing is a function of 21.____

    A. the ICN   B. the ANA
    C. state law   D. federal law

22. In order to resolve ethical dilemmas, a nursing staff should establish a sound database that will address each of the following questions EXCEPT: 22.____

    A. What is the patient's religious affiliation?
    B. What is the intent of the proposed action?
    C. What persons are involved in the situation?
    D. What are the possible consequences of the proposed action?

23. In 1914, 23.____

    A. the Thompson Practical Nursing School was founded in Brattleboro, Vermont
    B. the association of Practical Nursing Schools was founded

C. the Mississippi State Legislature was the first political body to pass license laws controlling practical nurses
D. Galen Health Institutes, Inc. opened practical/ vocational nursing programs in several states

24. When collecting data during the nursing process, a tertiary source of data would be

A. the patient himself
B. the patient's record
C. data from family and friends of the patient
D. the nurse's observations

25. Which of the following is an example of public law affecting nurses?

A. Sexual assault
B. Americans with Disabilities Act
C. Malpractice
D. Living wills

KEY (CORRECT ANSWERS)

1. D   11. A
2. B   12. B
3. C   13. B
4. C   14. D
5. C   15. B

6. D   16. C
7. B   17. B
8. D   18. C
9. B   19. A
10. A   20. B

21. C
22. A
23. C
24. B
25. A

TEST 3

DIRECTIONS: Each question or incomplete statement is followed by several suggested answers or completions. Select the one that BEST answers the question or completes the statement. *PRINT THE LETTER OF THE CORRECT ANSWER IN THE SPACE AT THE RIGHT.*

1. The CHIEF goal of a nurse in the role of care provider is to

   A. execute planned nursing interventions
   B. convey understanding of about what is important, and to provide support
   C. help the client to recognize and cope with stressful psychological or social problems
   D. prevent illness

2. Each of the following is characteristic of the process for developing critical pathways in a medical care facility EXCEPT

   A. a consensus is developed around the management of the case type by a multidisciplinary team that includes physicians
   B. information used includes insurance reimbursements
   C. before it becomes policy, a pathway is piloted in a clinical setting
   D. the process for developing a pathway is created independent of the agency

3. For legal purposes, the standards of care for nursing practice are most clearly defined by the

   A. NLN's Standards of Care
   B. ICN's Code of Ethics
   C. ANA's Code for Nurses
   D. state nurse practice act

4. Which of the following is a typical research function of a nurse at the associate degree level?

   A. Using nursing practice as a means of gathering data to refine and extend practice
   B. Reading, interpreting, and evaluating research for applicability to nursing practice
   C. Sharing research findings with colleagues
   D. Assisting in data collection within an established, structured format

5. According to the International Council of Nurses, the nurse's fundamental ethical responsibilities include the following EXCEPT to

   A. prevent illness
   B. sustain a cooperative relationship
   C. restore health
   D. alleviate suffering

6. A nurse who demonstrates marginally accepted performance is professionally categorized as

   A. a novice   B. an advanced beginner
   C. competent   D. proficient

7. A resident physician instructs nurses to order a complete blood count and urinalysis on all clients admitted to the emergency room and to get the results before calling him down. The nurses feel this is unethical; it is wasteful and causes discomfort and possible risks for the clients. Without having the authority to change the situation, however, they order the tests, feel guilty, and upset. This is an example of

    A. a decision-focused ethical problem
    B. an action-focused ethical problem
    C. intuitionism
    D. a deontological ethical problem

8. Each of the following has contributed to the professional nurse's increased role as a teacher EXCEPT

    A. new emphasis on health promotion
    B. increased client awareness
    C. shortened hospital stays
    D. increase in long-term illnesses and disabilities

9. According to Miller, the critical aspects of professionalism in nursing do NOT include

    A. delineating and specifying the skills and competencies that are the boundaries of expertise
    B. attaining a competence derived from the theoretical base
    C. gaining a body of knowledge in a university setting
    D. gaining a science orientation at the hospital level in nursing

10. When the American Society of Superintendents of Training Schools of Nursing was established in 1894, its primary goal was

    A. to promote the establishment of nursing education programs throughout the United States
    B. the increase in prestige and remuneration of civil nursing practice as compared to wartime nursing
    C. the establishment of educational standards for nursing
    D. recruitment and training of qualified nursing personnel

11. The general term for an expected standard of behavior for specific group members is

    A. folkway   B. law   C. rule   D. norm

12. It is NOT a purpose of nursing codes of ethics to

    A. give direction for actions to take in specific cases
    B. remind nurses of the special responsibility they assume when caring for the sick
    C. provide a sign of the profession's commitment to the public it serves
    D. guide the profession in self-regulation

13. _____ stimuli are most immediate to a patient, and precipitate certain observed behaviors.

    A. Focal   B. Contextual
    C. Residual   D. Primary

14. Since 1965, health care costs in the United States have increased by approximately 14._____

    A. 100% B. 200% C. 400% D. 600%

15. Before a civil trial, written answers to written questions, known as _____, are submitted by all parties. 15._____

    A. discoveries B. depositions
    C. affidavits D. interrogatories

16. In what year were the Medicare amendments to the Social Security Act adopted? 16._____

    A. 1945 B. 1955 C. 1965 D. 1975

17. Which of the following is a type of therapeutic intervention? 17._____

    A. Educating B. Monitoring
    C. Inspecting D. Observing

18. Which of the following is NOT typically involved in a nurse's responsibility as witness to a client's informed consent? 18._____

    A. Witnessing the client's signature
    B. Witnessing the exchange between the client and the physician
    C. Establishing that the client fully understands
    D. Securing the approval of a patient's living relation

19. Of the following, which patient value is most threatened by health care situations? 19._____

    A. Equity B. Security C. Autonomy D. Well-being

20. Which of the following is a secondary health care agency? 20._____

    A. Hospice B. Crisis center
    C. Long-term care facility D. Hospital

21. Which of the following is NOT an important priority of data collection during the assessment phase of the nursing process? 21._____

    A. Communicating with the client, rather than consulting secondary sources
    B. Including information about both strengths and needs
    C. Arranging results in a way easily retrievable by future researchers
    D. Including the client's responses to current alterations

22. Which of the following was the creator of nursing's *four conservation principles*? 22._____

    A. Neuman B. Orem C. Levine D. Rogers

23. Which of the following is not an essential element of nursing diagnosis? 23._____

    A. Focusing on person's responses
    B. Labeling conclusions
    C. Suggesting interventions
    D. Representing an opinion

24. Each of the following is a recommendation offered by the ANA regarding *do not resuscitate* (DNR) orders EXCEPT

    A. the wishes of the client's spouse and family must always take precedence
    B. when the client is incompetent, an advance directive or the surrogate decision-makers should make treatment decisions
    C. if it is contrary to the nurse's personal beliefs to carry out a DNR order, the nurse should consult the nursing manager for a change in assignment
    D. a DNR order is separate from other aspects of a client's care, and does not imply that other types of care should be withdrawn

25. The scientific method is useful in nursing research for

    A. applying research principles into real-world practice
    B. overcoming current inabilities to measure most concepts of interest to nurses
    C. to find answers to clinical problems
    D. helping to answer ethical or value questions

KEY (CORRECT ANSWERS)

1.	B	11.	D
2.	D	12.	A
3.	D	13.	A
4.	D	14.	C
5.	B	15.	D
6.	B	16.	C
7.	B	17.	A
8.	B	18.	D
9.	D	19.	C
10.	C	20.	D

21.	C
22.	C
23.	D
24.	A
25.	C

EXAMINATION SECTION
TEST 1

DIRECTIONS: Each question or incomplete statement is followed by several suggested answers or completions. Select the one that BEST answers the question or completes the statement. *PRINT THE LETTER OF THE CORRECT ANSWER IN THE SPACE AT THE RIGHT.*

1. The official accrediting body for programs in nursing is the

    A. National League for Nursing (NLN)
    B. American Medical Association (AMA)
    C. United Nursing League (UNL)
    D. American Nurses' Association (ANA)

1.____

2. The MINIMUM formal education that would be required for the position of Assistant Director of Nursing, Intensive Care Unit, is normally

    A. A.D.
    B. B.S.N.
    C. M.S.
    D. M.S.N. with two years' related experience

2.____

3. Which of the following is NOT a typical legal liability affecting nursing practice?

    A. Forgery
    C. Larceny
    B. Malpractice
    D. Battery

3.____

4. Each of the following is considered to be an advantage associated with associate nursing degree programs EXCEPT

    A. available to part-time students
    B. preparation for administrative roles
    C. relatively diverse student population
    D. efficient use of time

4.____

5. Which of the following would be considered grounds for false imprisonment charges to be filed against a nurse?

    A. Threatening to strike a patient
    B. Failing to protect a patient from injury
    C. Restraining a patient
    D. Performing blood tests on a patient without the patient's consent

5.____

6. The National Council Licensure Examination, or NCLEX, examines a candidate's knowledge of client needs along each of the following dimensions EXCEPT

    A. physical integrity
    B. effective care environment
    C. effective treatment plan
    D. health promotion/maintenance

6.____

7. All of the following may be used as reasons for revoking a nursing license EXCEPT

    A. emotional problems
    B. drug addiction
    C. acts that endanger the public
    D. incompetence

8. What is the term used to designate the curriculum track followed by students in a baccalaureate program who have received their basic education through an AD or diploma program?

    A. Elective
    B. Matriculated
    C. Articulated
    D. Core

9. What is the MINIMUM formal education that would usually be required for the position of Oncology Nursing Coordinator?

    A. A.D.
    B. B.S.N.
    C. M.A.
    D. M.P.H., with B.S. in nursing

10. R.N.s who return to school for a B.S.N. or M.S.N. degree should consider all of the following factors EXCEPT

    A. prior knowledge and patterns of thought
    B. differences in age and lifestyle
    C. present ability to supervise and evaluate
    D. acquired socializations

11. Formal recognition of a nurse's demonstration of competency by professional organizations or institutions (and not by state or federal boards) is termed

    A. credentialing
    B. certification
    C. licensure
    D. accreditation

12. Professional nursing practice requires, as a minimum level of education, a(n)

    A. associate degree
    B. nursing diploma
    C. baccalaureate degree
    D. master's degree

13. What is the MINIMUM formal education that would be required for the position of Nursing Instructor, Associate Degree Program?

    A. A.D.
    B. B.S.N.
    C. M.S. in psychiatric or medical-surgical nursing
    D. Any M.S.N. with two years' work experience

14. Candidates who plan to take either the SAT or ACT should register AT LEAST _____ in advance.

    A. six months
    B. three months
    C. six weeks
    D. three weeks

15. For purposes of litigation, standard of care is determined by all of the following EXCEPT   15.____

    A. specialty care associations
    B. emergency room statistics
    C. manuals
    D. agency policies

16. Which of the following is NOT a designation given by the American Nurses' Association?   16.____

    A. R.N., C.   B. R.N., C.S.
    C. C, R.N., C.N.A.A.   D. R.N., F.A.A.N.

17. Of the following, an ADVANTAGE associated with nursing diploma programs is   17.____

    A. accelerated level of patient contact
    B. that it offers transfer-level nursing courses
    C. qualification for most non-hospital positions
    D. diverse student population

18. What is the MINIMUM formal education that would usually be required for the position of Clinical Specialist?   18.____

    A. A.D.
    B. B.S.N.
    C. M.S. in field of specialty
    D. M.S.N. with two years' related experience in field of specialty

19. In choosing a nursing school, it is desirable to select a program affiliated with hospitals that have been approved by the   19.____

    A. NLN   B. AMA   C. AHA   D. JCAHO

20. The legal concept describing commonly accepted measures of competence and action on the part of medical professionals is termed   20.____

    A. nursing process
    B. standard of care
    C. interdependent intervention
    D. baseline competency

21. What is the MINIMUM formal education that would usually be required for the position of Clinical Nursing Coordinator?   21.____

    A. B.S.N.
    B. B.S.N. with five years' related clinical experience
    C. M.A.
    D. M.S.N.

22. The legal term for failure to act in a thoughtful manner, which results in harm to another, is   22.____

    A. defamation   B. assault
    C. malpractice   D. negligence

23. In which of the following organizations is membership composed of both nurses and non-nurses?   23.____

    A. ANA   B. AANA   C. AORN   D. NLN

24. Each of the following is an advantage associated with baccalaureate nursing programs EXCEPT   24.____

    A. preparation for leadership roles in community health
    B. broad general education requirements
    C. lower relative cost
    D. demanding curriculum

25. In order to avoid litigation, verbal or telephone orders from a physician should be signed within _____ hours.   25.____

    A. 10   B. 18   C. 24   D. 48

KEY (CORRECT ANSWERS)

1. A   11. B
2. C   12. C
3. C   13. C
4. B   14. C
5. C   15. B

6. C   16. D
7. A   17. A
8. C   18. C
9. D   19. D
10. C   20. B

21. B
22. D
23. D
24. C
25. C

TEST 2

DIRECTIONS: Each question or incomplete statement is followed by several suggested answers or completions. Select the one that BEST answers the question or completes the statement. *PRINT THE LETTER OF THE CORRECT ANSWER IN THE SPACE AT THE RIGHT.*

1. What is the MINIMUM formal education that would usually be required for the position of Director, School of Nursing (baccalaureate)? 1._____

    A. M.S.N.
    B. M.S.N. with five years' experience
    C. M.S.N. with ten years' experience
    D. Ph.D.

2. Of the following terms used in recognizing a nurse's demonstration of competency, _____ is MOST commonly applied in nursing. 2._____

    A. credentialing   B. certification
    C. licensure   D. accreditation

3. Currently, MOST nurses obtain R.N. status through completion of a(n) 3._____

    A. diploma program   B. associate degree
    C. baccalaureate degree   D. master's degree

4. Which of the following is NOT one of the fifteen areas of nursing practice that is offered certification by the American Nurses' Association? 4._____

    A. Adult nurse practitioner
    B. Clinical specialist in community health nursing
    C. High-risk perinatal nurse
    D. Clinical specialist in child and adolescent psychiatric and mental health nursing

5. A student in a master's program must USUALLY complete _____ units of academic study, in addition to 8 units of graduate professional work. 5._____

    A. 18-24   B. 24-30   C. 30-36   D. 36-45

6. The MINIMUM formal education that would usually be required for the position of Director, Home Health Agency, is the 6._____

    A. B.S.N.   B. M.S.N.   C. M.P.H.   D. Ph.D.

7. What is the legal term GENERALLY used to describe any form of professional misconduct? 7._____

    A. Malpractice   B. Incompetence   C. Negligence   D. Corruption

8. A candidate in an R.N. diploma program will USUALLY take _____ years to complete requirements. 8._____

    A. 1-2   B. 2-3   C. 4   D. 4 or more

9. Technical nursing practice requires a(n) _____ as a MINIMUM level of education.

   A. high school diploma
   B. associate degree
   C. baccalaureate degree
   D. master's degree

10. Which of the following mechanisms for controlling the quality of professional practice has NO legal status?

    A. Credentialing
    B. Certification
    C. Licensure
    D. Accreditation

11. A candidate who takes the College Level Examination Program (CLEP) General Examination can eliminate some tuition costs by earning as many as _____ semester hours of undergraduate credit.

    A. 12   B. 24   C. 30   D. 36

12. In legal terms, a written communication that damages a person's reputation is specifically known as

    A. defamation   B. slander   C. assault   D. libel

13. Each of the following is considered to be a disadvantage associated with practical nursing programs EXCEPT

    A. little upward mobility
    B. relative difficulty in qualifying for hospital work
    C. limited working capacity
    D. narrowly specialized education requirements

14. What is the MINIMUM formal education that would be required for the position of Visiting Staff Nurse?

    A. A.D.   B. B.S.N.   C. M.S.   D. M.S.N. or M.P.H.

15. Which of the following types of nursing practice does NOT require completion of either a nursing diploma or an associate degree?

    A. L.P.N.   B. M.S.N.   C. R.N.   D. C.C.R.N.

16. All of the following are considered to be grounds for filing assault and battery charges against a nurse EXCEPT

    A. performing urine tests without the patient's consent
    B. coercing patients into an unwanted treatment
    C. detaining a patient in an institution
    D. moving a protesting patient

17. The MINIMUM formal education that would be required for the position of Head Nurse CCU is

    A. A.D.
    B. B.S.N.
    C. M.S.
    D. M.S.N. with two years' related clinical experience

18. Which of the following is considered to be a disadvantage associated with baccalaureate nursing programs?

    A. Initial cost
    B. Limited qualification for non-hospital positions
    C. Limited student population
    D. Difficulty advancing to graduate study

19. Which of the following mechanisms for controlling the quality of professional practice is implemented through the use of state board examinations and state-approved schools of nursing?

    A. Credentialing
    B. Certification
    C. Licensure
    D. Accreditation

20. For purposes of litigation, the standard of care might be determined by

    A. expert witnesses
    B. NCLEX test scores
    C. institutional statistics
    D. patient testimony

21. From the time a student graduates from a school of nursing until he or she becomes licensed, the nurse works in the capacity of

    A. a licensed practical nurse
    B. a graduate nurse under a state-issued permit
    C. an undergraduate nurse under a limited institutional permit
    D. nurse's assistant

22. Of the following, one of the fifteen areas of nursing practice that is offered certification by the American Nurses' Association is

    A. gynecological nurse practitioner
    B. radiological nurse
    C. family nurse practitioner
    D. gastrointestinal nurse

23. The National Council Licensure Examination, or NCLEX, identifies all of the following as the five main behaviors that make up the nursing process EXCEPT

    A. prescribing
    B. planning
    C. assessing
    D. evaluating

24. The MINIMUM formal education that would be required for the position of Visiting Nurse Clinical Specialist is the

    A. A.D.
    B. B.S.N.
    C. M.S.
    D. M.S.N. with two years' related clinical experience

25. Affirmation that a school of nursing has requested evaluation and successfully met criteria established by the state board of registered nursing is termed

    A. credentialing
    B. certification
    C. licensure
    D. accreditation

KEY (CORRECT ANSWERS)

1. D
2. A
3. B
4. B
5. C

6. C
7. A
8. B
9. B
10. B

11. C
12. D
13. B
14. B
15. A

16. C
17. B
18. A
19. C
20. A

21. B
22. C
23. A
24. C
25. D

EXAMINATION SECTION
TEST 1

DIRECTIONS: Each question or incomplete statement is followed by several suggested answers or completions. Select the one that BEST answers the question or completes the statement. *PRINT THE LETTER OF THE CORRECT ANSWER IN THE SPACE AT THE RIGHT.*

1. Each nursing supervisor should work with his or her head nurses to determine the staff requirement for each unit. They should consider all of the following EXCEPT the _____ of the unit.

    A. past experiences
    B. anticipated needs
    C. length or size
    D. percentage of occupancy

2. The estimation of staff for each unit does NOT need to include

    A. provisions for vacations
    B. sick leave
    C. overtime pay
    D. on-call pay

3. Problems of cost increase of primary nursing could be overcome by the practice of

    A. assessing present staffing to bring it to an acceptable standard of patient care hours
    B. upgrading positions as vacancies occur
    C. utilizing all levels of staff more effectively
    D. all of the above

4. The _____ forecasting method employs the upside/downside concept and seeks to project realistic figures based on the impact of demands for services.

    A. mechanical   B. analytical   C. historic   D. qualitative

5. Critical factors to be considered in forecasting are future events or conditions that will affect

    A. situation
    B. people
    C. time
    D. all of the above

6. If you notice or experience price variance in supplies, you should determine the

    A. reasons causing price increase and whether the price increase is permanent or temporary
    B. availability of substitute supplies
    C. feasibility of reducing price through the bidding process or other purchase techniques
    D. all of the above

7. Manager education regarding the control of resources should involve all of the following EXCEPT

    A. salary education
    B. financial education
    C. responsibility
    D. accountability

8. To educate a manager regarding accountability, one should NOT

   A. clarify accountability
   B. provide positive support
   C. provide consistent feedback
   D. fail to enforce accountability

9. The fundamental elements of the nursing delivery system include

   A. clinical decision making
   B. work allocation
   C. communication
   D. all of the above

Questions 10-16.

DIRECTIONS: Answer Questions 10 through 16 using the following choices:

   A. Functional system
   B. Case system
   C. Primary care system
   D. Team system

10. The OLDEST method of delivering nursing care is the _____.

11. The MOST frequently adopted method of delivering nursing care is the _____.

12. The MOST recently developed nursing care delivery method is the _____.

13. One nurse is involved in nursing observation and care of a single patient. This system of delivering nursing care is termed the _____.

14. The nursing care delivery system that focuses on the number of tasks that must be provided to the overall patient population is called the _____.

15. When different members of the nursing staff do tasks for a given patient, they employ the _____.

16. The MOST comprehensive care, in terms of patient's need, is BEST provided by the _____.

17. The objectives of team nursing include providing

   A. adequate staff for good care
   B. good experiences for staff members
   C. good personnel policies to maintain morale
   D. all of the above

18. The case system of delivering nursing care is PRIMARILY used for assignments in the

   A. outpatient clinic   B. inpatient clinic
   C. intensive care unit   D. home

19. In the primary care delivery system, the _____ make(s) the final decision about nursing care of assigned patients.

    A. team leader
    B. primary nurse
    C. head nurse
    D. different nurses

20. A team member, as a part of team nursing, should do all of the following EXCEPT

    A. when reporting for duty, obtain a written assignment
    B. receive verbal or taped reports on the team's patients
    C. plan care for the next shift
    D. take orders from nursing care plans and doctor's order sheet

21. Of the following, the one which does NOT have to be considered when making team nursing assignments is

    A. ethnic background of patients
    B. qualitative work load
    C. quantitative work load
    D. geography of unit

22. The primary nurse is a registered professional nurse, responsible and accountable for all of the following EXCEPT

    A. the nursing process for a specified number of patients
    B. delivery of care 24 hours a day from admission to discharge
    C. all patients in the given unit
    D. participation in a communication triad between patient and physician

23. Which of the following is NOT among the key points regarding primary care nursing?

    A. Continuity of patient care
    B. Accountability to peers, the patient, and the physician
    C. Role model for the patient
    D. Patient inclusion in planning care

24. The cooperative care system of nursing

    A. allows the patient to maintain a passive role, receiving assistance and guidance from health care professionals
    B. has patient education as its primary therapeutic tool
    C. eliminates the need for professional nurses, eventually
    D. suggests that a home-like environment is not therapeutic to a patient's convalescence

25. In the cooperative care model, the staff nurses MUST possess

    A. a registered nurse license
    B. a wide knowledge of various medical and surgical specialties
    C. excellent communication skills
    D. all of the above

KEY (CORRECT ANSWERS)

1. C		11. A	
2. C		12. C	
3. D		13. B	
4. B		14. A	
5. D		15. A	
6. D		16. C	
7. B		17. D	
8. D		18. C	
9. D		19. B	
10. B		20. C	

21. A
22. C
23. C
24. B
25. D

———

TEST 2

DIRECTIONS: Each question or incomplete statement is followed by several suggested answers or completions. Select the one that BEST answers the question or completes the statement. *PRINT THE LETTER OF THE CORRECT ANSWER IN THE SPACE AT THE RIGHT.*

1. All of the following are components of nursing case management EXCEPT

    A. accountability for the clinical and financial outcomes of patients' entire episodes of care
    B. the use of a caregiver as a case manager
    C. formal RN-MD group practices
    D. none of the above

1._____

2. Paramount to the nursing care management model is the use of

    A. formal RN-MD group practices
    B. the caregiver as a case manager
    C. increased patient and family participation in and control of health care
    D. accountability

2._____

3. Increased patient and family participation in and control of health care is achieved by

    A. pre- and post-hospitalization phone calls
    B. giving patients copies of their critical paths
    C. negotiating meaningful outcomes and discharge plans
    D. all of the above

3._____

4. The case manager is NOT expected to

    A. establish a mechanism for notification when a new patient enters the caseload
    B. complete a follow-up evaluation
    C. begin assessment, set goals, and make plans independent of the physician
    D. introduce self to the patient or family and explain the role of case manager and group practice

4._____

5. Potential benefits of differentiated nursing practice include all of the following EXCEPT

    A. effective deployment of nursing staff into emerging new roles
    B. decreased demand for physicians
    C. increased clinical management skills
    D. shared governance that facilitates staff nurse involvement in the clinical decision-making process

5._____

6. Cooperative care is a method of delivering nursing care to patients who

    A. require intensive care
    B. need 24 hour a day nursing observation
    C. do not require intensive or 24 hour a day observation
    D. come to the hospital for day surgery

6._____

7. Guidelines for designing nursing forms include:

   A. Determine the purpose of the form
   B. Identify benefits that will be derived from introduction of the form into the record
   C. Design the form as simply as possible
   D. All of the above

8. _____ does NOT affect nursing staffing.

   A. Characteristics of staff
   B. Ethnicity and racial background of staff and patients
   C. Trends in nursing care delivery
   D. The presence of unionization

9. The suggested nurse/patient ratio for ALL shifts, 24 hours a day, 7 days a week, in cooperative care nursing is 1:

   A. 8   B. 4   C. 2   D. 1

10. In the cooperative care nursing delivery system, a nurse coordinator has all of the following support persons EXCEPT a(n)

    A. associate director of nursing
    B. assistant nurse coordinator
    C. physician
    D. unit manager

11. The direct link between the coordinator in the cooperative care system and the executive director of nursing services and other hospital administrators is the

    A. assistant director of nursing
    B. associate director of nursing
    C. unit manager
    D. medical director

12. All of the following are components of the nursing care process EXCEPT

    A. assessment and planning   B. implementation
    C. education   D. evaluation

13. Assessment components of the nursing care process include all of the following EXCEPT

    A. history   B. treatment
    C. physical examination   D. nursing diagnosis

14. The functions of the planning component of the nursing care process include

    A. assigning priority to the problem diagnosed
    B. differentiating problems
    C. designating specific actions
    D. all of the above

15. The planning phase begins with

    A. nursing diagnosis
    B. assessment
    C. development of nursing care plans
    D. evaluation

16. The planning phase of the nursing care process terminates with

    A. nursing diagnosis
    B. development of nursing care plans
    C. implementation
    D. evaluation

17. The development of a nursing care plan is the blueprint for

    A. action
    B. providing direction for implementing the plan
    C. providing the framework for evaluation
    D. all of the above

18. Once a nursing care plan has been developed, _____ begins.

    A. evaluation
    B. assessment
    C. implementation
    D. accountability

19. The implementation component of the nursing care process draws heavily on _____ nursing skills.

    A. intellectual
    B. interpersonal
    C. technical
    D. all of the above

20. Significant skills that enhance the success of the implementation component of the nursing care process include all of the following EXCEPT

    A. decision making
    B. social attitude
    C. observation
    D. communication

21. The INCORRECT statement regarding the evaluation component of nursing care is: It

    A. is expressed in terms of expected behavioral manifestations within the client
    B. indicates the degree to which the nursing diagnosis and nursing actions have been correct
    C. does not help to diagnose any new problems
    D. helps the nurse and the client to determine which problems have been resolved and which need to be reprocessed

22. A nursing diagnosis which focuses on a patient is a

    A. physiological condition combined with a problem
    B. pathophysiological response to a problem
    C. physical or behavioral response to a problem
    D. verbal response to a disease process

23. ADVANTAGES of nursing diagnoses include 23.____
    A. assisting in organizing, defining, and developing nursing knowledge
    B. facilitating the evaluation of the nursing process
    C. focusing nursing care on the patient's responses to problems
    D. all of the above

24. For effective utilization of a nursing care plan, it is important to 24.____
    A. clearly define nursing care objectives
    B. have supportive policies
    C. have administrative support
    D. all of the above

25. The successful development and carrying out of a nursing care plan for a patient 25.____
    depends upon knowledge of all of the following EXCEPT the patient's

    A. financial status   B. background
    C. personality   D. illness

KEY (CORRECT ANSWERS)

1. D	11. B
2. B	12. C
3. D	13. B
4. C	14. D
5. B	15. A
6. C	16. B
7. D	17. D
8. B	18. C
9. A	19. D
10. C	20. B

21. C
22. C
23. D
24. D
25. A

EXAMINATION SECTION
TEST 1

DIRECTIONS: Each question or incomplete statement is followed by several suggested answers or completions. Select the one that BEST answers the question or completes the statement. *PRINT THE LETTER OF THE CORRECT ANSWER IN THE SPACE AT THE RIGHT.*

1. In evaluating the timing *of* an activity and sequencing the alternatives, a management team at a nursing home should determine the *critical path* through the nursing home's network. The critical path in this context is the element of the activity which

   A. takes the longest to complete
   B. takes the shortest time to complete
   C. requires the most resources
   D. requires the fewest resources

   1.____

2. Which of the following most accurately states the growing trend in the structuring of the nursing home industry?

   A. Greater proportional reliance on public financing
   B. Consolidation into larger health care organizations
   C. Greater reliance on extended-care facilities
   D. Dispersement into smaller community-level facilities

   2.____

3. According to most health care professionals and executives, the most ethically troubling aspects of the Medicaid program is that

   A. recipients must prove their eligibility in accord with the program's provisions
   B. many elderly transfer their assets to children in order to make themselves eligible
   C. taxes from working people are used to provide services to elderly beneficiaries
   D. states are subject to federal regulations in the apportionment of benefits

   3.____

4. Studies of nursing homes have generally indicated that a low percentage of private-pay patients in a nursing facility

   A. is a negative indicator of the quality of care
   B. more typically occurs in urban facilities
   C. usually leads to a greater reliance on physical restraints
   D. may increase the degree to which a facility is subject to federal regulation

   4.____

5. Which of the following payors is/are usually involved in fixed reimbursement programs?
   I. Medicare
   II. Medicaid
   III. Blue Cross
   IV. Commercial third-party insurer

   The CORRECT answer is:

   A. I, II   B. I, III
   C. II, III, IV   D. II, IV

   5.____

6. Studies indicate that the MOST common process deficiency in United States nursing homes is

   A. an inadequate care plan
   B. a hazardous environment
   C. unsanitary food
   D. the improper use of restraints

7. The effect of the prospective payment system for Medicare, established in 1983, was to

   A. provide a cost-based approach to reimbursement
   B. establish fixed rates for each Medicare admission by diagnosis
   C. regulate the way in which long-term care institutions competed against each other for market share
   D. establish a new system of organizational review for all health care institutions

8. Most staff experience has shown that the activity with which residents are most likely to need assistance is

   A. eating
   B. dressing
   C. getting in or out of a chair
   D. bathing

9. Federal regulations require nursing facilities to complete minimum data set (MDS) forms for patients within _____ of admission.

   A. 48 hours   B. 14 days   C. 30 days   D. 3 months

10. In most nursing homes, daily life is permeated by a model of staff-resident relationships that is most clearly drawn from

    A. child-care settings
    B. client-centered professions such as law
    C. acute-care medical settings
    D. municipal government and constituents

11. Which of the following were effects of the 1983 introduction of Medicare's Prospective Payment System (PPS)?
    I. Overall decreases in long-term care costs
    II. More flexibility in long-term care reimbursement procedures
    III. More referrals and admissions to nursing facilities
    IV. Early discharge from acute care facilities

    The CORRECT answer is:

    A. I, II   B. II, III   C. III, IV   D. I, IV

12. Nationwide, what is the average total number of nursing care hours per resident day in Medicaid-only facilities?

    A. 1   B. 2   C. 3   D. 4

13. Which of the qualitative techniques for decision analysis attempts to optimize the distribution of scarce resources among competing activities? 13.____

    A. Queuing theory
    B. Regression analysis
    C. Linear programming
    D. Network analysis

14. How many hours of in-service training for nursing assistants is currently required each year by federal regulations? 14.____

    A. 0   B. 12   C. 40   D. 64

15. Which of the following is NOT a trend currently taking place in the demographics of United States health care clients? 15.____

    A. Increasing poverty
    B. A rapidly changing racial and ethnic composition due to immigration and growing minority populations
    C. A trend toward smaller family size
    D. An increase in the percentage of younger clients

16. Which of the following factors are affected by the patient mix at a nursing home? 16.____
    I. Staffing
    II. Service mix
    III. The way in which quality-of-care indicators should be interpreted
    IV. Regulations affecting nursing home activities and staffing
    The CORRECT answer is:

    A. I, II
    B. II, IV
    C. I, II, III
    D. I, III

17. Which of the following is a difference between professional review organizations (PROs) and the older professional standards review organizations (PSROs) established by federal health care regulations? 17.____

    A. PROs are made up of solely not-for-profit, physician-sponsored groups.
    B. PROs are paid by federal grants.
    C. PSROs involve smaller geographic areas.
    D. PSROs were subject to the Freedom of Information Act (FOIA)

18. A nursing home administrator or director of nursing at a nursing home can expect the leading cause of illness or injury among nursing assistants to be 18.____

    A. strains and sprains, mostly involving the back
    B. slips or falls to a lower level
    C. respiratory infection
    D. needlestick injuries

19. The largest association for long-term care facilities in the United States is the 19.____

    A. Group Health Association of America (GHAA)
    B. American Hospital Association (AHA)
    C. Federation of American Hospitals (FAH)
    D. American Health Care Association (AHCA)

20. Of the following aspects of nursing home life, the one most exclusively characteristic of United States facilities is the

    A. housing of residents in shared rooms
    B. degree to which physical and chemical restraints are used
    C. use of geriatric or gerontological nursing staff
    D. attempt to involve family members in formulating a care plan

21. Overall, out-of-pocket contributions from clients now accounts for about _____ % of all expenditures on nursing home care in the United States.

    A. 11   B. 22   C. 33   D. 44

22. Compared to nonprofit nursing homes, for-profit facilities generally tend to

    A. have substantially fewer staff
    B. provide better quality care to Medicaid beneficiaries and self-pay residents
    C. have fewer adverse outcomes from pressure sores
    D. make substantially greater use of physical restraints

23. Which of the following is an element of the bureaucratic model of management?

    A. Interdepartmental collaboration
    B. Positions arranged in a matrix
    C. Generalization of tasks
    D. A consistent system of abstract rules

24. Which of the following is the professional society to which a nursing home executive would belong?

    A. American College of Health Executives (ACHE)
    B. American Health Care Administration (AHCA)
    C. Accrediting Commission on Education for Health Services Administration (ACE-HSA)
    D. American Public Health Administration (APHA)

25. Of the following generalizations about nursing home residents, the CORRECT one is that about

    A. 75% are female
    B. 20% are chairbound
    C. 75% are bladder incontinent
    D. 20% require tube feeding

26. The types of managerial decisions made at organizations such as health care facilities typically include each of the following EXCEPT

    A. programmed-nonprogrammed
    B. inclusive-exclusive
    C. administrative-operational
    D. ends-means

27. Gerontological nurse specialists (GNSs) and geriatric nurse practitioners (GNPs) can improve resident outcomes in nursing facilities by
    I. increasing the ability of a facility to care for more complex and acutely ill patients
    II. reducing the use of hospital services
    III. changing the focus from custodial to rehabilitative care
    IV. reducing the incidence of resident behaviors requiring physical restraint
    The CORRECT answer is:

    A. I, II
    B. II, III
    C. III, IV
    D. I, II, III, IV

28. Studies indicate that the LEAST common outcome deficiency in United States nursing homes is

    A. poor nutrition
    B. resident abuse
    C. failure to prevent pressure sores
    D. inadequate treatment of incontinence

29. Nursing homes which make extensive use of urinary catheters should be aware that the practice increases the risk of each of the following undesirable outcomes EXCEPT

    A. abscesses
    B. urinary tract infection
    C. malnutrition
    D. renal failure

30. Programs for cognitively impaired residents in nursing homes should include
    I. music
    II. space set aside where movements will not disturb others
    III. periods of unstructured activity
    IV. small, confined spaces
    The CORRECT answer is:

    A. I, II
    B. II, III
    C. III, IV
    D. I, IV

KEY (CORRECT ANSWERS)

1.	A	16.	C
2.	B	17.	C
3.	B	18.	A
4.	A	19.	D
5.	B	20.	B
6.	C	21.	C
7.	B	22.	B
8.	D	23.	D
9.	B	24.	A
10.	C	25.	A
11.	C	26.	B
12.	C	27.	D
13.	C	28.	B
14.	B	29.	C
15.	D	30.	A

TEST 2

DIRECTIONS: Each question or incomplete statement is followed by several suggested answers or completions. Select the one that BEST answers the question or completes the statement. *PRINT THE LETTER OF THE CORRECT ANSWER IN THE SPACE AT THE RIGHT.*

1. Which of the following is NOT a provision of the Omnibus Budget Reconciliation Act of 1987 (OBRA 87)? 1.____

    A. Nursing homes were encouraged to shift the focus of care from custodial to rehabilitative care.
    B. State Medicaid programs were encouraged to adjust their rates.
    C. Nursing homes were encouraged to develop a resident assessment program for every patient upon discharge.
    D. Nursing homes receiving federal funds were required to ensure a high quality of life in addition to a high quality of care.

2. Which of the following is an element of a *functional* organization, as opposed to a *project* organization? 2.____

    A. Superior-subordinate boundaries are less clear.
    B. Line functions have direct responsibility for accomplishing objectives.
    C. Prime emphasis is placed on horizontal and diagonal work flow.
    D. Management is a joint venture of many relatively independent organizations.

3. Which of the demographic sectors is most clearly on the increase among nursing home residents? 3.____

    A. Males
    B. Those over the age of 85
    C. Those with chronic cognitive impairment
    D. Married couples

4. Since 1988, which of the following types of nursing professionals have experienced the smallest percentage increase in nursing homes? 4.____

    A. Geriatric nurse practitioners
    B. Nursing assistants
    C. Registered nurses
    D. Licensed practical nurses

5. Which of the following is NOT typically a difficulty involved in the use of surrogate decision-makers for cognitively impaired residents? 5.____

    A. The lack of a formally appointed guardian but several de facto guardians
    B. Illegal or unethical decisions made by a guardian
    C. Difficulty in reversing guardianships once cognitive functions are regained
    D. Difficulty in delineating the scope of decision-making for a guardian

6. Which of the following reasons best explains why many nursing home administrators are reluctant to invest in the training of nursing assistants?

   A. Extensive use of part-time staff
   B. High turnover rates
   C. Adequate supervision and instruction by supervising nurses
   D. High nursing assistant-to-bed ratio

7. Which of the following management roles pertains to the effort to establish suitable organizational objectives and to implement plans capable of accomplishing them?

   A. Decisional
   B. Strategist
   C. Informational
   D. Designer

8. Which of the qualitative techniques for decision analysis derives a mathematical equation to describe or express the relationship between the data of two or more variables over a period of time?

   A. Queuing theory
   B. Regression analysis
   C. Linear programming
   D. Network analysis

9. Which of the following is MOST likely to be a characteristic associated with a resident in a nursing facility?

   A. Receiving psychoactive medications
   B. Physical restraints
   C. Bladder incontinence
   D. Bedfast

10. Which of the following are acceptable means by which the staff at a nursing facility can assure respect for the autonomy of cognitively impaired residents?
    I. Advance directives
    II. Asking residents for permission before performing any procedure
    III. Surrogate decision makers
    IV. The use of restraints to insure safety
    The CORRECT answer is:

    A. I only
    B. II, IV
    C. I, III
    D. II, III

11. In cases where the use of physical and chemical restraints are an issue for a resident, the course of action is usually dictated by

    A. the will of the resident's family
    B. the will of the resident
    C. the judgment of the nursing staff
    D. state regulations

12. Which of the following comparisons of fee-for-service (FFS) and managed care (HMO) nursing care is generally TRUE?

    A. Managed care enrollees are more satisfied with their paperwork requirements.
    B. FFS enrollees are more satisfied with their plan's cost.
    C. Managed care enrollees make greater use of their plan's services.
    D. FFS enrollees are less satisfied with their quality of care.

13. Though advance directives have proven helpful in some cases involving the care of cognitively impaired residents, the practice suffers from the significant difficulty of

    A. compliance with federal and state regulations
    B. frequent conflicts with the facility's formal care policies
    C. family members who step in after the fact to combat the carrying-out of directives
    D. delineating the areas of decision for which advance directives should have force

14. Each of the following is considered to be an element of the internal management function of a nursing home administrator EXCEPT

    A. evaluating, training, and developing management personnel
    B. developing and improving management information systems
    C. determining and establishing priorities for new services
    D. defining the general course and goal priorities for the organization

15. The current Medicaid floor for a resident's personal-needs allowance is

    A. $30 a month   B. $75 a month
    C. $1,000 a year   D. $3,000 a year

16. The 1987 Nursing Home Reform Act provides that nursing assistants must be certified and that they must receive _____ hours of training within the first _____ months of employment in order to be certified.

    A. 10; 2   B. 40; 2   C. 75; 4   D. 120; 4

17. Approximately what percentage of skilled-nursing facilities in the United States have 24-hour coverage by at least one registered nurse?

    A. 30   B. 50   C. 70   D. 85

18. The staff at a nursing home has become so overwhelmed with requests for IV feedings that it has to postpone several scheduled sessions. In brainstorming about the possible reasons why feedings could not meet demand, the management team decides to first list all the possible explanations.
    Which of the following visual tools would best help the team to do this?

    A. Decision tree
    B. Pareto diagram
    C. Payoff table
    D. Ishikawa (fishbone) diagram

19. According to many staff surveys, the main problem associated with the federal nursing home regulations issued by the Omnibus Budget Reconciliation Act of 1987 (OBRA 87) is that

    A. they focus too much on the rehabilitative aspects of care
    B. the time involved in satisfying documentation requirements detracts from the quality of care
    C. the costs of satisfying staffing requirements decrease the likelihood of profitability
    D. they set an unrealistic standard of care for nursing staff

20. In the 1990s, the type of long-term care facilities which experienced the highest growth rate were

    A. nursing facilities
    B. home care agencies
    C. residential care facilities
    D. adult day care agencies

21. Which of the following is considered an outcome variable involved in nursing home care?

    A. Assessment frequency and completeness
    B. Mortality
    C. Use of restraints
    D. Staffing mix

22. The factor which most clearly distinguishes the long-term care market from the hospital market is the

    A. role of private insurance and Medicare
    B. financial status of the clients who utilize services
    C. demand for services
    D. impact of public welfare on expenditures

23. The *second generation* of federal nursing home regulations, issued during the 1990s, tended to focus primarily on

    A. discriminatory admission practices
    B. resident autonomy and respect for rights
    C. safety
    D. reimbursement

24. The purpose of CON legislation, passed in nearly all states by 1983, was to

    A. regulate the amounts charged by health care facilities
    B. divide professional review organizations into their geographic areas of jurisdiction
    C. provide all nonprofessional and paramedical workers in health care organizations with the same workplace hazard protections as doctors and nurses
    D. force institutional health care providers to obtain state approval for construction or renovation projects beyond a certain cost

25. Which of the following is a likely consequence of the shortage of available nursing home care in many states?

    A. More flexible CON requirements at the state level
    B. Greater selectivity in nursing home admission practices
    C. An increasing focus on the individuals with the greatest need for services
    D. An increase in extended care facilities

KEY (CORRECT ANSWERS)

1. C	11. A
2. B	12. A
3. B	13. D
4. B	14. C
5. B	15. A
6. B	16. C
7. B	17. B
8. B	18. D
9. C	19. B
10. C	20. C

21. B
22. A
23. B
24. D
25. B

EXAMINATION SECTION
TEST 1

DIRECTIONS: Each question or incomplete statement is followed by several suggested answers or completions. Select the one that BEST answers the question or completes the statement. *PRINT THE LETTER OF THE CORRECT ANSWER IN THE SPACE AT THE RIGHT.*

1. According to Freudian theory, the _____ functions to encourage a person's tolerance of frustration.   1.____

    A. subconscious   B. id
    C. ego   D. superego

2. Which of the following hormones controls the use of glucose by the body's cells?   2.____

    A. Cortisone   B. Insulin
    C. Adrenal steroids   D. Thyroxine

3. A client who is receiving lithium carbonate should undergo regular monitoring of   3.____

    A. blood pressure   B. blood level
    C. weight   D. urine

4. According to intrapsychic theory, the problem of separation anxiety is MOST likely to occur during the _____ stage.   4.____

    A. latency   B. oral   C. anal   D. phallic

5. A client with adrenal insufficiency is weak and dizzy upon arising in the morning. The MOST likely cause of this is   5.____

    A. lack of sodium
    B. increased intracavity fluid volume
    C. hypertension
    D. hypoglycemic reaction

6. The administration of Anectine prior to electroconvulsive therapy involves the major complication of   6.____

    A. loss of bowel control
    B. inhibition of breathing muscles
    C. memory loss
    D. the bite reflex

7. An infant with congenital hyperthyroidism is at risk for _____ if care is not given immediately.   7.____

    A. thyrotoxicosis   B. acromegaly
    C. myxedema   D. mental retardation

8. For which of the following is lithium carbonate used as a control or modifier?   8.____

    A. Manic episode of bipolar disorder
    B. Acute agitation of schizophrenia

C. Agitated phase of paranoia
D. Depressive phase of major depression

9. Which of the following is the cause of acromegaly?

   A. Oversecretion of adrenal steroids
   B. Undersecretion of thyroid hormone
   C. Oversecretion of growth hormone
   D. Undersecretion of testosterone

10. At what approximate age does a person demonstrate the primary emergence of his or her personality?

    A. 6 months B. 18 months
    C. 2 years   D. 8 years

11. Diabetic acidosis is caused by elevated _____ levels in the blood.

    A. lactic acid B. ketone
    C. albumin   D. glucose

12. Which of the following behaviors is MOST likely to be demonstrated by an autistic child?

    A. Lack of response to external stimuli
    B. Sad facial expression
    C. Irrelevant smiling
    D. Rocking and flapping of hands

13. To evaluate the effectiveness of DDAVP in treating diabetes insipidus, which of the following should be monitored?

    A. Blood pressure B. Intake and output
    C. Pulse rate   D. Serum glucose

14. Glucagon

    A. retards glycogenesis
    B. causes the release of insulin
    C. elevates blood sugar levels
    D. improves the storage of glucose

15. Of the following, the clearest evidence of mental illness is when a client

    A. does not seem to be able to complete tasks
    B. has difficulty relating to others
    C. has little interest in social activities or work
    D. encounters frequent periods of high anxiety

16. For a client with insulin-dependent diabetes mellitus, insulin needs will *decrease* when the client

    A. exercises   B. is infected
    C. reaches middle age D. is emotionally stressed

17. The treatment for a client suffering from depression should focus on getting the client to   17._____

    A. express anger toward others
    B. admit an emotional problem
    C. articulate feelings of low self-esteem
    D. accept care and comfort willingly

18. A child who is about to undergo surgery to correct a congenital megacolon should be given a preoperative enema of   18._____

    A. barium   B. isotonic saline
    C. tap water   D. hypertonic phosphate

19. Which of the following is a common side effect associated with the use of Thorazine?   19._____

    A. Jaundice   B. Melanocytosis
    C. Photosensitivity   D. Excessive thirst

20. Piaget's theory of cognitive development states that at the age of six months, an infant should demonstrate   20._____

    A. a sense of time
    B. the ability to remember
    C. the onset of object permanence
    D. coordinated motor responses

21. Which of the following would MOST clearly reveal congenital hip dysplasia in a newborn infant?   21._____

    A. Different leg lengths
    B. Asymmetrical gluteal folds
    C. Limited adduction
    D. Skewed leg alignment

22. A client is diagnosed with an organic mental disorder. Which of the following nursing strategies would be MOST helpful to this client?   22._____

    A. Providing a diet high in carbohydrates
    B. Providing a variety of stimuli to keep the client's interest high
    C. Eliminating the need for choices
    D. Asking the client for input concerning the nursing care plan

23. Which of the following would be included in the early treatment of diabetic acidosis?   23._____

    A. IV fluids   B. Kayexalate
    C. Potassium   D. NPH insulin

24. Which level of consciousness BEST represents a person's feelings and attitudes?   24._____

    A. Conscious   B. Unconscious
    C. Preconscious   D. Foreconscious

25. What is the MOST common cause of diabetic ketoacidosis?

    A. Inadequate fluid intake
    B. Psychological stress
    C. Elevated insulin level
    D. Infection

KEY (CORRECT ANSWERS)

1.	C	11.	B
2.	C	12.	D
3.	B	13.	B
4.	B	14.	C
5.	D	15.	B
6.	B	16.	A
7.	D	17.	A
8.	A	18.	B
9.	C	19.	C
10.	C	20.	C

21. B
22. C
23. A
24. B
25. D

TEST 2

DIRECTIONS: Each question or incomplete statement is followed by several suggested answers or completions. Select the one that BEST answers the question or completes the statement. *PRINT THE LETTER OF THE CORRECT ANSWER IN THE SPACE AT THE RIGHT.*

1. A client with an anxiety disorder is likely to handle the anxiety in each of the following ways EXCEPT

    A. projecting it onto nonthreatening objects
    B. converting it into a physical symptom
    C. demonstrating regressive behavior
    D. acting out with antisocial behavior

    1.____

2. What type of diet is recommended for a client with Graves' disease?

    A. High roughage
    B. Low sodium
    C. Liquid
    D. High-calorie

    2.____

3. Which of the following is the cause of primary degenerative dementia?

    A. Anatomic brain changes
    B. Atrophy of the frontal lobes
    C. An extended history of malnutrition
    D. Excessive use of narcotics

    3.____

4. Which of the following blood gas results would indicate diabetic acidosis?

    A. Reduced HCO_3
    B. Elevated pH
    C. Reduced PO_2
    D. Elevated PCO_2

    4.____

5. The primary difference between a psychophysiologic disorder and a somatoform disorder is that a

    A. psychophysiologic disorder involves an actual change in tissues
    B. somatoform disorder is caused by emotions
    C. psychophysiologic disorder restricts the client's activities
    D. somatoform disorder is accompanied by a feeling of illness

    5.____

6. Which of the following is MOST likely to be a complication following the insertion of a ventriculoperitoneal shunt in a child with communicating hydrocephalus?

    A. Violent tremors
    B. Distended abdomen
    C. Yellowish discharge from shunt
    D. Fever

    6.____

7. Each of the following is a common physiological response to anxiety EXCEPT

    A. respiratory constriction
    B. dilated pupils
    C. hyperglycemia
    D. increased pulse rate

    7.____

8. It is MOST important for a nurse to monitor a client suffering from alcohol and cirrhosis for

   A. gastric pain
   B. blood in the stool
   C. dizziness
   D. constipation

9. To encourage a withdrawn and noncommunicative client to talk, the BEST nursing plan would include the attempt to

   A. ask the client to describe feelings
   B. ask simply-phrased questions that require yes or no answers
   C. join the client in an activity that the client enjoys
   D. concentrate on subjects that are nonthreatening

10. What is the function of glucose in a cell?

    A. Energy extraction
    B. Protein synthesis
    C. Cellular respiration
    D. Genetic coding

11. Which of the following treatments would be included in a plan for a client with severe and intractable depression and suicidal tendency?

    A. High doses of tranquilizers
    B. Electroconvulsive therapy
    C. Nondirective psychotherapy
    D. Thorazine

12. A *decrease* in the anterior pituitary secretion of ACTH would be caused by

    A. ketosis
    B. a *decrease* in the blood concentration of adrenal steroids
    C. an *increase* in the blood concentration of cortisol
    D. acidosis

13. A client is experiencing a phase of extreme elation and hyperactivity. Which of the following nursing interventions would BEST meet the client's nutritional needs?

    A. Assuming that the client will eat when hungry
    B. Firmly suggesting that the client sit and eat the meal that has been prepared
    C. Inducing an IV feeding to insure that the client is properly nourished
    D. Giving the client frequent high-calorie feedings that the client can feed to herself

14. Which of the following would be experienced by a client with acute cholecystitis accompanied by biliary colic?

    A. Melena
    B. Lipid intolerance
    C. Diarrhea
    D. Pain in lower left quadrant

15. Which of the following must be monitored especially closely following a hypophysectomy?

    A. Motor reflexes
    B. Urinary output
    C. Intracranial pressure
    D. Respiration

16. Which of the following would MOST accurately characterize the personality of a client with obsessive-compulsive personality disorder?

    A. Deep depression
    B. Indecisiveness and doubt
    C. Rapid mood swings
    D. Detailed delusions

17. Which of the following symptoms would MOST likely be revealed during an assessment of a client with Cushing's syndrome?

    A. Dehydration
    B. Migraine headaches
    C. Menorrhagia
    D. Hypertension

18. Most commonly, the behavior of a client with schizophrenia can be described as

    A. euphoric
    B. angry and hostile
    C. flat and apathetic
    D. depressed

19. Which of the following medications would be used to treat a child with cystic fibrosis?

    A. Antimetabolite
    B. Pancreatic enzymes
    C. Fat-soluble vitamins
    D. Aerosol mists

20. Which of the following would NOT be a helpful component of a nursing care plan for a severely depressed client?

    A. Short-term projects
    B. Client participation in activity planning
    C. Repetitive activities
    D. Simple instructions to be followed

21. A client with Addison's disease is experiencing hypotension. Most likely, this involves a disturbance in the production of

    A. mineralocorticoids
    B. proteins
    C. glucocorticoids
    D. insulin

22. Which of the following medications would be used to counter an overdose of narcotics?

    A. Methadone
    B. Thorazine
    C. Benzedrine
    D. Narcan

23. Prior to a serum glucose test, a client with Type II diabetes mellitus should

    A. have a clear liquid breakfast
    B. take prescribed medications
    C. void the bladder
    D. avoid food and fluids

24. Which of the following is the BEST description of a somatoform disorder? A(n)

    A. conscious defense against stress
    B. sublimation of stress
    C. psychological defense against anxiety
    D. unconscious means of controlling conflict

25. Which of the following tests is conducted to detect PKU in infant children?   25._____

   A. OCT
   C. BUN
   B. Phenistix test
   D. Guthrie blood test

KEY (CORRECT ANSWERS)

1. D
2. D
3. B
4. A
5. A

6. D
7. A
8. B
9. D
10. A

11. B
12. C
13. D
14. B
15. C

16. B
17. B
18. C
19. B
20. B

21. A
22. D
23. D
24. D
25. D

TEST 3

DIRECTIONS: Each question or incomplete statement is followed by several suggested answers or completions. Select the one that BEST answers the question or completes the statement. *PRINT THE LETTER OF THE CORRECT ANSWER IN THE SPACE AT THE RIGHT.*

1. A client recently admitted to an alcohol detoxification unit would probably exhibit each of the following EXCEPT   1.____

    A. hypertension
    B. nausea
    C. hyperactivity
    D. loss of appetite

2. Prior to an adrenalectomy, the client should   2.____

    A. increase fluid intake
    B. receive steroids
    C. have all medication withheld for 48 hours
    D. be placed on a high-protein diet

3. A client with an antisocial personality disorder   3.____

    A. learns quickly through experience and punishment
    B. is generally unable to defer gratification
    C. often masks his disorder by articulate communication
    D. suffers from a high level of anxiety

4. Which of the following is a defense mechanism that helps an individual channel unacceptable desires into socially approved behavior?   4.____

    A. Regression
    B. Denial
    C. Conversion
    D. Sublimation

5. Which of the following would NOT be a likely result of a laboratory test performed on a client suffering from diabetic ketoacidosis?   5.____

    A. Low CO_2
    B. Increased acidity
    C. High bicarbonate
    D. Increased blood sugar

6. Following an adrenalectomy, a client is MOST likely to exhibit the symptoms of   6.____

    A. sodium retention
    B. dehydration
    C. hypotension
    D. increased urinary output

7. It is MOST important for a nurse to _____ when attempting to resolve a crisis situation with a client.   7.____

    A. encourage socialization
    B. meet all of the client's dependency needs
    C. nurture the client's ego strengths
    D. introduce the client to a therapy group

8. Which of the following is NOT a typical indication of a hypoglycemic reaction to insulin?   8.____

    A. Paleness
    B. Excessive thirst
    C. Tremors
    D. Perspiration

83

9. A client is admitted to the hospital with a diagnosis of conversion disorder. The nurse should expect the client's attitude toward his physical symptoms to be one of

   A. hysteria
   B. indifference
   C. anger
   D. great sadness

10. Along with vitamin D, the regulatory agent that controls the overall calcium balance in the body is

    A. parathyroid hormone
    B. growth hormone
    C. thyroid hormone
    D. ACTH

11. A client is admitted to the hospital with Wernicke's encephalopathy caused by chronic alcoholism. The client's initial treatment would include

    A. an increase in fluid intake
    B. IM injection of thiamine
    C. administration of an anti-opiate
    D. administration of paraldehyde

12. Each of the following is a defect commonly associated with tetralogy of Fallot EXCEPT

    A. pulmonary artery stenosis
    B. mitral valve stenosis
    C. right ventricular hypertrophy
    D. overriding aorta

13. Which of the following statements, spoken to a nurse by a patient diagnosed with Alzheimer's disease, would indicate a need to accomplish Erikson's developmental task of ego integrity versus despair?

    A. I don't understand why I have to go through this.
    B. Please leave me alone.
    C. I can take care of myself.
    D. I am useless to everyone now.

14. The purpose of administering Mycifradin to a client with liver disease is to

    A. increase the urea digestive activity of enteric bacteria
    B. protect the liver from bacteria
    C. reduce ammonia-forming bacteria in the intestinal tract
    D. aid the digestion of complex proteins

15. Emotionally disturbed children

    A. seem unresponsive to their environment
    B. respond equally to all stimuli
    C. respond violently to most stimuli
    D. are immersed in their environment to the point of distraction

16. A client exhibiting cold intolerance may have

    A. increased levels of CO_2
    B. decreased blood pH

C. insufficient bile salts
D. decreased levels of T_3 and T_4

17. The part of the psyche that develops from internalizing the concepts of parents and other significant relations is the

    A. foreconscious
    B. id
    C. ego
    D. superego

18. Which of the following is NOT a typical sign of hypo-kalemia?

    A. Weakness
    B. Abdominal distention
    C. Edema
    D. Apathy

19. Which of the following might be experienced by a person who makes an abrupt withdrawal from habitual use of barbiturates?

    A. Gastric bleeding
    B. Cardiac arrhythmia
    C. Convulsions
    D. Ataxia

20. Which of the following would be observed in a toddler with cyanotic congenital heart disease?

    A. Orthopnea
    B. Blotchy skin
    C. Increased hematocrit
    D. Pitting edema

21. A delusional client is admitted for psychiatric treatment after harming a close relative. In talking about the incident, the client refers to herself in the third person. This is an example of the defense mechanism of

    A. conversion
    B. transference
    C. dissociation
    D. displacement

22. Which of the following is the clearest indication of diabetes insipidus?

    A. Elevated blood glucose
    B. Increased blood pressure
    C. Decreased urinary specific gravity
    D. Increased BUN

23. Which of the following is the MOST common cause of functional mental illness?

    A. Infection
    B. Chemical imbalance
    C. Social environment
    D. Genes

24. Which gland regulates the rate of oxygenation in the body's cells?

    A. Thyroid
    B. Adrenal
    C. Thalamus
    D. Pituitary

25. Which of the following is NOT thought to be a significant formative component of personality?

    A. Cultural setting
    B. Genetic background
    C. Psychologic development
    D. Biologic constitution

KEY (CORRECT ANSWERS)

1. C
2. B
3. B
4. D
5. C

6. C
7. C
8. B
9. B
10. A

11. B
12. B
13. D
14. C
15. A

16. D
17. D
18. C
19. C
20. C

21. C
22. B
23. C
24. A
25. B

TEST 4

DIRECTIONS: Each question or incomplete statement is followed by several suggested answers or completions. Select the one that BEST answers the question or completes the statement. *PRINT THE LETTER OF THE CORRECT ANSWER IN THE SPACE AT THE RIGHT.*

1. The preservation of sodium in the body's cells is accomplished by the hormone

    A. parathyroid hormone
    B. thyrocalcitonin
    C. aldosterone
    D. insulin

2. Which of the following behaviors would be LEAST likely to be demonstrated by a client with an organic mental disorder?

    A. An inclination to ignore the present circumstances while dwelling in the past
    B. A steadfast resistance to change
    C. The inability to focus on new interests
    D. A fixation on personal appearance and hygiene

3. Which of the following is a complication associated with hyperparathyroidism?

    A. Bone destruction
    B. Graves' disease
    C. Hypotension
    D. Tetany

4. Which of the following interventions should be undertaken to prevent thrombus formation in a client with sickle-cell anemia?

    A. Administer heparin or other anticoagulants
    B. Encourage exercise
    C. Maintain a high-roughage diet
    D. Increase oral fluid intake

5. A client with an obsessive-compulsive personality disorder will MOST likely react with _____ if he is interrupted in the performance of a ritual.

    A. hostility
    B. indifference
    C. confusion
    D. withdrawal

6. Which of the following would be experienced by a patient in a diabetic coma, but not by a patient in an HHNK coma?

    A. Kussmaul respirations
    B. Glycosuria
    C. Fluid loss
    D. Elevated blood glucose

7. Which of the following daily patterns tends to work best with clients who are depressed?

    A. Numerous sensory stimuli
    B. A simple daily schedule
    C. Removing the need for complicated decisions
    D. Multiple and varied activities

8. Glucocorticoids are secreted by the

    A. hypophysis cerebri
    B. adrenal glands
    C. thyroid
    D. pancreas

9. Prior to beginning lithium carbonate therapy, a client should undergo

   A. fluid and electrolyte evaluation
   B. renal evaluation
   C. psychomotor
   D. BUN evaluation

10. Which of the following is the result of an underproduction of thyroxin?

    A. Acromegaly
    B. Cushing's disease
    C. Myxedema
    D. Addison's disease

11. Which of the following is a common side effect of the major tranquilizers?

    A. Tremors
    B. Diaphoresis
    C. Jaundice
    D. Photosensitivity

12. Each of the following is likely to be revealed during the assessment of a client with hyperthyroidism EXCEPT

    A. weight loss
    B. increased appetite
    C. constipation
    D. nervousness

13. Severe emotional disturbances are often treated with tranquilizers to

    A. prevent complications
    B. make the client less dangerous to himself and others
    C. improve the client's mood
    D. make the client more receptive to psychotherapy

14. Which of the following symptoms would cause a nurse to stop giving Thorazine to a client?

    A. Uncoordinated movements
    B. Jaundice
    C. Withdrawal
    D. Tremors

15. What is the MOST likely cause of ascites in a patient with cirrhosis?

    A. Inhibited portal venous return
    B. Undersecretion of bile salts
    C. Gastric bleeding
    D. Overproduction of serum albumin

16. The defense mechanism used by clients who express anxiety through physical symptoms can BEST be described as

    A. psychosomatic
    B. regressive
    C. psychoneurotic
    D. dissociative

17. A 42-year-old client is admitted to the hospital with a diagnosis of Addison's disease. She is weak, hypotensive, and has low sodium and high potassium levels.
    The focus of the client's therapy should be

    A. lowering the level of eosiniphils
    B. restoring electrolyte balance
    C. increasing carbohydrate intake
    D. increasing lymph

18. A client who has been hospitalized for major depression has recently begun to receive Parnate. It is important that the nurse explain to the client that the use of this drug

    A. typically causes extreme photosensitivity
    B. may cause drowsiness
    C. increases the heart rate
    D. involves dietary restrictions

19. The MOST frequent cause of Cushing's syndrome is

    A. hyperplasia of pituitary
    B. hyperplasia of adrenal cortex
    C. decreased adrenocortical hormones
    D. insufficient production of ACTH

20. A group setting is particularly conducive to therapy because it

    A. takes the focus off the individual client
    B. forces clients to notice similarities with others
    C. establishes a learning environment
    D. encourages individual relationships

21. What is the purpose of installing a T-tube after a cholecystectomy?

    A. Draining bile from the cystic duct
    B. Protecting the common bile duct
    C. Preventing infection
    D. Providing a port for cholangiogram dye

22. A nurse notices that a socially agressive elderly client, who has been receiving Thorazine for several months, is sitting rigidly in a chair. What other adverse effects of the drug should the nurse watch for?

    A. Tremors
    B. Slurred speech
    C. Excessive salivation
    D. Withdrawal

23. For what reason is an infant born with a cleft palate prone to infection?

    A. Mouth breathing
    B. Leakage of nasal mucus
    C. Poor nutrition from feeding disturbances
    D. Poor circulation in defective locus

24. Which of the following is a defense mechanism in which emotional conflicts are expressed through sensorimotor or somatic disability?

    A. Dissociation
    B. Conversion
    C. Displacement
    D. Regression

25. For the emergency treatment of ketoacidosis, what type of insulin should be administered? 25.____

   A. Zinc suspension
   B. NPH insulin
   C. Protamine zinc suspension
   D. Regular insulin injection

KEY (CORRECT ANSWERS)

1. C
2. D
3. A
4. D
5. A

6. A
7. B
8. D
9. B
10. C

11. A
12. C
13. D
14. B
15. A

16. C
17. B
18. D
19. B
20. C

21. B
22. A
23. A
24. B
25. D

EXAMINATION SECTION
TEST 1

DIRECTIONS: Each question or incomplete statement is followed by several suggested answers or completions. Select the one that BEST answers the question or completes the statement. *PRINT THE LETTER OF THE CORRECT ANSWER IN THE SPACE AT THE RIGHT.*

1. You are assisting with the care of a patient who is suffering from false sensory perceptions and is completely out of touch with reality. These perceptions are referred to as
    A. visions
    B. delusions
    C. hallucinations
    D. flashbacks

2. A suicidal patient needs assistance to the bathroom. How should you act when dealing with this situation?
    A. Closely observe the patient
    B. Allow the patient privacy while in the bathroom
    C. Permit the patient to shave
    D. Make sure all sharp items have been removed from the room

3. Which of the following is important when caring for a patient with anorexia nervosa?
    A. Allow the patient to have privacy during meal times
    B. Patients should adhere to a strict meal plan
    C. No visitors should be permitted until the patient begins to eat normally
    D. You should be present at all times to make sure the patient eats

4. A recently widowed woman is dealing with severe depression and is possibly suicidal. Which of the following questions would be appropriate in order to determine whether or not the patient is suicidal?
    A. "Why do you want to kill yourself?"
    B. "How would you kill yourself?"
    C. "Are you sure you want to kill yourself?"
    D. "Where would you kill yourself?"

5. Which of the following characteristics would be evident for a patient who is abusing opiates such as morphine?
    A. Euphoria and dilated pupils
    B. High energy and dilated pupils
    C. Anger and constricted pupils
    D. Slurred speech and dilated pupils

6. What is the appropriate action when a patient is having an anxiety attack?
    A. Stay with the patient and speak calmly and slowly
    B. Open windows and turn on lights to avoid claustrophobia
    C. Leave the patient alone in silence
    D. Turn on soothing music

7. If a patient has delusions of grandeur, what does this refer to?
   A. The patient feels that he/she is extremely important
   B. The patient is experiencing hallucinations
   C. The patient is suicidal
   D. The patient is severely depressed

8. Enforcing limits on behavior is most important for what type of patient?
   A. Depressed
   B. Suicidal
   C. Anxious
   D. Manic

9. What are signs and symptoms of post-traumatic stress disorder?
   A. Hostility and violence
   B. Behavior changes and anorexia
   C. Hyper alertness and insomnia
   D. Memory loss and insomnia

10. Which of the following is appropriate for a patient with manic depression?
    A. Encouraging the patient to eat high calorie meals
    B. Insisting on highly exertional activities so patient sleeps at night
    C. Listening closely and avoiding power struggles
    D. Allowing patient to behave with no limits

11. A patient with post-traumatic stress disorder is experiencing nightmares, depression, alcohol abuse, and feelings of hopelessness. Which of the following is important for relieving the symptoms of this patient?
    A. Regular attendance at Alcoholics Anonymous meetings
    B. Family support
    C. Proper anti-anxiety medicine
    D. Encouraging patient to talk about the past experiences

12. If a patient is undergoing detoxification for a heroin overdose and states they can stop using heroin if they want to is an example of which coping mechanism?
    A. Repression
    B. Delusion
    C. Denial
    D. Withdrawal

13. What is a common characteristic among patients who suffer from dependent personality disorder?
    A. Cannot form lasting relationships
    B. Cannot make decisions without seeking advice
    C. Self-destructive behavior
    D. Hopelessness

14. Which of the following is an early sign of alcohol withdrawal?
    A. Slurred speech
    B. Perceptual disorders
    C. Agitation
    D. Depression

15. Which of the following is a characteristic of a patient with schizotypal personality disorder when faced with a social situation?
    A. Paranoia
    B. Depression
    C. Agitation
    D. Homicidal impulses

16. When a patient is in a manic state, what is the MOST appropriate action to relieve this situation?
    A. Encourage patient to express feelings
    B. Discourage interaction with other people until manic state passes
    C. Encourage interaction with others to relieve manic state
    D. Reduce any stimulation that may contribute to the manic state

17. Which of the following is imperative in order to care for a patient with bulimia?
    A. Determine which situations cause anxiety
    B. Determine why the patient feels they need to lose weight
    C. Determine what foods the patient likes to eat
    D. Restrict patients to three planned meals per day

18. Which of the following behaviors is indicative of adult cognitive development?
    A. Generating new levels of awareness
    B. Assuming responsibility for actions
    C. Can solve problems and learn new skills
    D. Has reality-based perceptions

19. Which of the following is common when a patient first begins to take lithium for treatment of bipolar disorder?
    A. Excessive thirst
    B. Excessive urination
    C. Constipation
    D. Excessive hunger

20. What characteristics are common for a patient who has overdosed on amphetamines?
    A. Low pulse rate
    B. Low blood pressure
    C. Slurred speech
    D. Irritability

21. Which medications are appropriate for treating patients who commonly suffer from panic attacks?
    A. Opiates
    B. Anti-depressants
    C. Anti-anxiety medications
    D. Barbiturates

22. What is the BEST course of action when a patient is actively having hallucinations that are causing agitation?
    A. Try to bring the patient back to reality
    B. Give the patient a sedative
    C. Try to find out the content of the hallucination
    D. Immediately restrain the patient

23. What is the BEST course of action when a patient with paranoid schizophrenia gets upset and tells you to leave him alone?
    A. Explain that you are in control, not the patient
    B. Continue to do your job regardless of the patient's feelings
    C. Explain that you will leave for now but be back soon
    D. Find out why the patient wants to be left alone

24. What condition is characterized by tonic contractures of the muscles of the neck, mouth, and tongue?
    A. Dystonia
    B. Dyskinesia
    C. Heroin overdose
    D. Cocaine overdose

    24.____

25. Which blood electrolyte level is important to monitor before a patient begins to take lithium?
    A. Potassium   B. Sodium   C. Calcium   D. Chloride

    25.____

KEY (CORRECT ANSWERS)

1.	C	11.	D
2.	A	12.	C
3.	B	13.	B
4.	B	14.	B
5.	D	15.	A
6.	A	16.	D
7.	A	17.	A
8.	D	18.	A
9.	C	19.	B
10.	C	20.	D

21. C
22. C
23. C
24. A
25. B

TEST 2

DIRECTIONS: Each question or incomplete statement is followed by several suggested answers or completions. Select the one that BEST answers the question or completes the statement. *PRINT THE LETTER OF THE CORRECT ANSWER IN THE SPACE AT THE RIGHT.*

1. Which of the following is defined as the state of well-being where a person can realize his own abilities and cope with normal stresses of life and work?
    A. Mental illness
    B. Mental health
    C. Physical health
    D. Emotional health

1.____

2. Which duty is appropriately performed by a mental health technician?
    A. Administering medications to a patient
    B. Coordinating the overall care for a patient
    C. Providing information regarding alcohol abuse
    D. Prescribing medications for treatment of a patient

2.____

3. If a patient states, "Give me a few minutes to remember," this patient is operating on which of the following?
    A. Conscious
    B. Subconscious
    C. Unconscious
    D. Ego

3.____

4. Which of the following is a characteristic of the superego portion of the psyche?
    A. It is the censoring portion of the mind
    B. It is impulsive and lacks morals
    C. It analyzes prior to making decisions
    D. It uses defensive functions for protection

4.____

5. Which of the following characteristics is associated with the primary level of prevention?
    A. Rehabilitating a patient to take care of himself
    B. Making sure a suicidal patient cannot harm himself
    C. Performing community-wide disease surveillance
    D. Teaching a patient how to deal with stress

5.____

6. If you suspect a woman and a child are victims of abuse, which of the following questions is MOST appropriate for you to ask?
    A. "Are you okay?"
    B. "Is something bothering you?"
    C. "What happened to you?"
    D. "Are you being threatened or hurt by your partner?"

6.____

7. Sexual _____ disorder would be characterized by a female abuse victim who develops a diminished sex drive.
    A. pain
    B. arousal
    C. desire
    D. appetite

7.____

8. If a patient is still living with an abusive spouse, what is the BEST advice you can offer?
    A. Tell the patient to end the relationship
    B. Tell the patient to summon the family's opinion regarding the relationship
    C. Give the patient information for a crisis center
    D. Tell the patient what you would do if you were in the same situation

9. Which of the following statements could indicate child abuse if made by a parent?
    A. "If I tell my child to do something once, I better not have to tell them again."
    B. "My child tells me no all the time."
    C. "Once my child is potty trained, I can still expect an accident from time to time."
    D. "I encourage my children to try new and different things."

10. What is the PRIMARY concern when dealing with a victim of child abuse?
    A. Understand why the child is being abused
    B. Make sure the patient is safe from further harm
    C. Make sure the patient is now comfortable
    D. Teach the victim how to mentally deal with the abuse

11. Which somatoform disorder is characterized by constant complaints of pain or illness without any medical or clinical explanation?
    A. Hypochondriasis
    B. Conversion disorder
    C. Somatization disorder
    D. Somatoform Pain disorder

12. According to Sigmund Freud, anxiety is defined as
    A. conflict between the id and superego
    B. a hypothalamic-pituitary-adrenal reaction to stress
    C. a conditioned response to stress
    D. functions to satisfy the need for security

13. Which of the following medications would be appropriate for reducing the symptoms of alcohol withdrawal?
    A. Narcan   B. Librium   C. Haldol   D. Phenobarbital

14. Parents of children who develop anorexia nervosa commonly have which of the following characteristics?
    A. History of drug abuse
    B. Generally ignoring their children
    C. Tendency to be strict and overprotective
    D. Tendency to be extremely aggressive and goal oriented

15. What is the FIRST priority when dealing with a spousal abuse victim and the spouse shows up to *finish the job*?
    A. Confront the abusing spouse
    B. Remain with the victim and stay calm
    C. Call security and another staff member for assistance
    D. Ask the abusing spouse why this happened

16. Which aspect is very important when dealing with a patient with bulimia in which strict management of dietary intake is necessary?
    A. Allowing the patient to eat meals in private
    B. Allowing the patient to choose their own food and staying with them for an hour after the meal is finished
    C. Choosing the food for the patient and making sure they eat at least half of the meal
    D. Keeping patient engaged in activities for two hours after each meal time

17. Patients being treated with Antabuse need to carefully read the labels on which products to avoid potential reactions?
    A. Sodas
    B. Cologne and aftershaves
    C. Toothpaste
    D. Juices

18. If you are caring for an injured child, what specific action would lead you to believe the child is being abused?
    The child
    A. does not cry when being examined
    B. does not make eye contact with the caregiver
    C. cries uncontrollably throughout the examination
    D. resists contact from the caregiver

19. The patient's _____ needs is the highest priority when encountering a patient who has taken PCP.
    A. medical
    B. psychological
    C. physical
    D. safety

20. How would you proceed if you entered a room and found a patient sitting on the floor with cuts on both wrists and surrounded by broken glass?
    A. Approach the patient slowly, speak in a calm voice, call the patient by name and tell them you are here to help
    B. Move the glass away and sit down next to the patient
    C. Call for additional staff before entering the room and restraining the patient
    D. Enter the room quietly and get beside the patient to assess him

21. Clonidine is useful for treating which condition other than hypertension?
    A. Alcohol withdrawal
    B. Opiate withdrawal
    C. Cocaine withdrawal
    D. Heroin withdrawal

22. Which of the following are early signs of alcohol withdrawal?
    A. Sweating, tremors, nervousness
    B. Hypertension, sweating, seizures
    C. Dehydration, fever, itching
    D. Vomiting, diarrhea, slow heart rate

22.____

23. What are some behavioral characteristics for a person with antisocial personality disorder?
    A. Continuously talks of violence
    B. Silence and disobedient
    C. Rigid posture, restlessness, glaring
    D. Depression and physical withdrawal

23.____

24. How long after the last alcoholic drink will early withdrawal symptoms begin to become evident?
    A. 6 hours
    B. 12 hours
    C. 24-48 hours
    D. 60-72 hours

24.____

25. What is the proper treatment for a patient experiencing hallucinations secondary to alcohol abuse?
    A. Keep patient restrained until hallucinations stop
    B. Check blood pressure every 15 minutes and force fluids
    C. Keep environment calm and quiet and give medications as needed
    D. Continuously monitor the patient and check blood pressure every 30 minutes

25.____

KEY (CORRECT ANSWERS)

1.	B	11.	D
2.	A	12.	A
3.	B	13.	B
4.	A	14.	C
5.	D	15.	C
6.	D	16.	B
7.	C	17.	B
8.	C	18.	A
9.	A	19.	D
10.	B	20.	A

21.	B
22.	D
23.	C
24.	C
25.	C

EXAMINATION SECTION
TEST 1

DIRECTIONS: Each question or incomplete statement is followed by several suggested answers or completions. Select the one that BEST answers the question or completes the statement. *PRINT THE LETTER OF THE CORRECT ANSWER IN THE SPACE AT THE RIGHT.*

1. A patient tells you that the other patients are plotting to kill him. This is MOST likely an example of

    A. a manic-depressive reaction
    B. a paranoid reaction
    C. excellent perceptual skills on the part of the patient
    D. a compulsive reaction

2. Which of the following statements is TRUE?

    A. Diagnoses are, by their very nature, always accurate.
    B. Phobic reactions are the most common reasons people are admitted to mental hospitals.
    C. People with neuroses are far less likely to be hospitalized than people with psychoses.
    D. Severely depressed patients are less of a suicide risk than any other patient group, except paranoid schizophrenics.

3. The LARGEST single diagnostic group of psychotic patients are

    A. neurotic depressive
    B. schizophrenic
    C. obsessive-compulsive
    D. paranoid reactive

4. The personality type that would BEST be characterized by the description that *he or she has no conscience* would be the

    A. drug addict
    B. exhibitionist
    C. sociopath
    D. manic-depressive

5. Of the following, the marked inability to organize one's thoughts is found MOST commonly and severely in

    A. schizophrenics
    B. amnesiacs
    C. those suffering from anxiety neuroses
    D. sociopaths

6. Someone who constantly feels tense, anxious, and worried but is unable to identify exactly why is MOST likely to be suffering from

    A. anxiety neurosis
    B. schizophrenia
    C. dissociative reaction
    D. a conversion reaction

7. A patient always insists upon twirling around six times before entering a new room, or she fears she will die. This is an example of

    A. paranoid reaction
    B. obsessive-compulsive reaction
    C. dissociative reaction
    D. anxiety neurosis

8. Of the following, those who suffer from neuroses would USUALLY complain of

   A. rejections, dissociation, and frequent inability to remember what day it is
   B. delusions, rejections, and feeling tired
   C. tiredness, fears, and hallucinations
   D. fears, physical complaints, and anxieties

9. The category that is caused by a disorder of the brain for which physical pathology can be demonstrated is

   A. neurotic depressive reaction
   B. schizophrenia
   C. functional psychoses
   D. organic psychoses

10. Of the following, which is NOT true?

    A. Someone who is suddenly unable to hear for psychological reasons would be considered to be suffering from a conversion reaction.
    B. If someone is in fugue, they have combined amnesia with flight.
    C. *Multiple personalities* is a dissociative reaction that affects primarily the elderly.
    D. General symptoms of schizophrenia include an ability to deal with reality, the presence of delusions or hallucinations, and inappropriate affect.

11. Which one of the following is TRUE?

    A. Calling an elderly person *gramps* or *granny* makes them feel more secure.
    B. It is important for an elderly person to maintain his or her independence whenever possible.
    C. When elderly patients start acting like children, they should be treated like children.
    D. It is important to encourage the elderly to hurry because they tend to move so slowly.

12. It has been found that older patients learn BEST when one does all but which one of the following?

    A. Allowing plenty of time for them to practice and learn
    B. Creating a relaxing environment for them
    C. Dealing with one thing at a time
    D. Assuming little knowledge on their part

13. Which of the following contains the main factors that should be considered before administering medications to elderly patients?

    A. How popular the medication is with the patient and the team leader's recommendations
    B. Any organic brain damage, liver dysfunction, and body weight
    C. Liver dysfunction, the patient's medical history, and decreased body weight
    D. Decreased body weight, impaired circulation, liver dysfunction, and increased sensitivity to medications

14. When communicating with the hearing impaired, it is BEST to do all of the following EXCEPT

    A. make sure the person can see your lips
    B. speak slowly and clearly
    C. use gestures
    D. shout

15. The three most common visual disorders in the elderly are cataracts, diabetic retinopathy, and glaucoma.
    Of the following statements about these, the one that is NOT true is that

    A. the symptoms for cataracts are a need for brighter light and a need to hold things very near the eyes
    B. diabetic retinopathy, if untreated, can cause blindness, so any vision or eye problems in diabetics should be promptly reported
    C. glaucoma develops slowly, so it is much easier to detect than cataracts or diabetic retinopathy
    D. some of the symptoms of glaucoma are loss of vision out of the corner of the eye, headaches, nausea, eye pain, tearing, blurred vision, and halos around objects of light

16. Which of the following is NOT true?

    A. Most of the elderly hospitalized for psychiatric problems suffer from senile brain atrophy or brain changes that occur due to arteriosclerosis.
    B. It is important to allow the elderly who wish to, the right to always live in the past.
    C. The majority of the elderly are competent, alert, and functioning well in their communities.
    D. Many elderly patients feel that they are no longer valued members of our society.

17. Of the following, which is NOT a good reason for helping the elderly patient stay active? Activity

    A. promotes good health by stimulating appetite and regulating bowel function
    B. prevents the complications of inactivity such as pneumonia, bed sores, and joint immobility
    C. can create an interest in taking more medication
    D. can increase blood circulation

18. Staff members must come to an understanding of their own feelings about the elderly because

    A. the staff may then be more helpful
    B. any negative feelings one has may be difficult to hide
    C. feelings of fear or aversion can be easily transmitted
    D. all of the above

19. An elderly patient will probably eat better if

   A. food servings are large
   B. the foods are chewy
   C. he or she is allowed to finish his/her meals at a leisurely pace
   D. cooked food is served cold

20. The MOST common accident to the elderly involves

   A. falls   B. burns   C. bruises   D. cuts

21. Which of the following is TRUE?

   A. Children should be considered and treated as miniature adults.
   B. Children are growing, developing human beings who will react to situations according to their level of development and the experiences to which they have been subjected.
   C. Children who are brought to a mental health center are usually calm and non-apprehensive on their first visit.
   D. The problems of adolescents are usually overestimated.

22. In working with adolescents, it would be BEST to

   A. neither bend over backwards to give in to demands, nor control them by rigid and punitive means
   B. dress the way most adolescents do
   C. staff those units with young people
   D. watch television with them regularly

23. Of the following, when working with children, it is MOST important to be

   A. consistent
   B. strict
   C. more concerned for their welfare than for the welfare of the other patients
   D. well-liked

24. Of the following, the element that is MOST lacking in relationships between adolescents and adults is

   A. respect   B. fear   C. trust   D. sensitivity

25. Of the following, the BEST reason for grouping children together would be

   A. they should be protected from the influences of all adult patients
   B. children tend to feel more comfortable with other children
   C. children are less likely to *act out* when they are with other children
   D. they would be unable to bother adult patients

26. All of the following statements are true EXCEPT:

    A. Accidents, reactions to drugs, fevers, and disease may each contribute to mental or emotional problems
    B. How effectively an individual reacts to and manages stress contributes to his or her mental health
    C. There is significant research that indicates that mental illness is caused primarily by genetic transmittal
    D. A person's upbringing, his or her relationships with family or friends, past experiences, and present living conditions may all contribute to the status of his or her mental health

27. All of the following are basic psychological needs which must be met for a person to have self-esteem EXCEPT

    A. acceptance and understanding
    B. trust, respect, and security
    C. a rewarding romantic relationship
    D. pleasant interactions with other people

28. All of the following statements are true EXCEPT:

    A. Most people become mentally ill because they are unable to cope with or adapt to the stresses and problems of life
    B. People with emotional problems can rarely be helped enough to live independently
    C. Most of the diseases and symptoms of the body which plague people have a large emotional component as their cause
    D. Environmental and familial factors are more important than genetic factors in mental illness

29. The following are all optimal aspects of family functioning EXCEPT

    A. communication is open and direct
    B. expression of emotion is more often positive than negative
    C. minor problems are ignored, knowing they will go away on their own
    D. there is a high degree of congruence or harmony between the family's values and the actual realities of the society

30. All of the following statements are true EXCEPT:

    A. People who are wealthy rarely become mentally ill
    B. Physical disease may influence emotional balance
    C. People who are mentally ill are often very sensitive to what is happening in their environment
    D. Most people doubt their own sanity at one time or another

31. All of the following statements are true EXCEPT:

    A. Hereditary factors are not the primary cause of mental illness
    B. A person may react to an extremely traumatic experience by becoming mentally ill
    C. Early recognition and treatment does not affect the course of mental illness
    D. Mental illness can develop suddenly

32. All of the following statements are true EXCEPT:

    A. Emotionally disturbed people are usually very sensitive to how other people feel towards them
    B. People do not inherit mental disorders, but may inherit a predisposition to certain types of mental problems
    C. There are many factors which can cause mental illness
    D. Mood swings are signs of mental illness

33. Which of the following statements is LEAST accurate?

    A. The difference between being mentally healthy and mentally ill often lies in the intensity and frequency of inappropriate behavior.
    B. The way a person views a situation determines his or her response to the situation.
    C. The mentally ill are permanently disabled.
    D. Different personal experiences cause a difference in what a person perceives as stressful, and how much stress a person can tolerate.

34. All of the following statements are true EXCEPT:

    A. Most experts in the field of mental health believe that the experiences which occur during the first twenty, or the first six, years of life are the most significant
    B. An unfortunate characteristic of children is that they tend to blame themselves for failures of their parents, and thus may develop feelings of inadequacy which may affect them all of their lives
    C. If neglect is severe enough, an infant or young child may withdraw from reality into a fantasy world which feels less threatening
    D. Human beings develop in the exact same pattern and almost at the same rate

35. Schizophrenia is

    A. genetically caused
    B. most often caused by the habitual use of drugs
    C. the result of a complex relationship between biological, psychological, and sociological factors
    D. most commonly caused by the inhalation of toxic gases

KEY (CORRECT ANSWERS)

1.	B	16.	B
2.	C	17.	C
3.	B	18.	D
4.	C	19.	C
5.	A	20.	A
6.	A	21.	B
7.	B	22.	A
8.	D	23.	A
9.	D	24.	C
10.	C	25.	B
11.	B	26.	C
12.	D	27.	C
13.	D	28.	B
14.	D	29.	C
15.	C	30.	A

31. C
32. D
33. C
34. D
35. C

TEST 2

DIRECTIONS: Each question or incomplete statement is followed by several suggested answers or completions. Select the one that BEST answers the question or completes the statement. *PRINT THE LETTER OF THE CORRECT ANSWER IN THE SPACE AT THE RIGHT.*

1. Tardive dyskenesia is a(n)

    A. antidepressant
    B. birth-related serious injury
    C. serious side effect of phenothiazine derivatives
    D. antiparkinsons drug

    1.____

2. People taking psychotropic drugs are MOST likely to be sensitive to

    A. long exposures to sunlight
    B. darkness
    C. noise
    D. other patients

    2.____

3. An antipsychotic drug that is a phenothiazine derivative would MOST likely be used for

    A. helping a patient lose weight
    B. calming a patient
    C. helping a patient sleep
    D. reducing the frequency of delusions in a patient

    3.____

4. Of the following, an antidepressant such as Elavil would MOST likely be used for

    A. the immediate prevention of suicidal action in a newly admitted patient
    B. helping a patient lose weight
    C. elevating a patient's mood
    D. diuretic purposes

    4.____

5. Which of the following statements is NOT true?

    A. Antianxiety tranquilizers such as sparine, librium, and vistaril are useful primarily with psychoneurotic and psychosomatic disorders.
    B. Minor or antianxiety tranquilizers tend to be less habit-forming than major or antipsychotic tranquilizers.
    C. Akinesia, pseudoparkinsonism, and tardive dyskenesia are serious side effects of antipsychotic drugs, or phenothiazine derivatives.
    D. Generally, those using tranquilizers like sparine or librium are in less danger of deadly drug overdoses than those using barbituates.

    5.____

6. All of the following statements are false EXCEPT:

    A. Antipsychotic drugs promote increased sexual interest
    B. Patients no longer need to take their medication when they feel better
    C. Phenothiazines are psychotropic drugs
    D. One of the main difficulties with antipsychotic drugs is that they tend to be habit-forming

    6.____

7. Yellowing of the skin or eyes, sensitivity to light and pseudoparkinsonism may occur in patients receiving

    A. mellaril or thorazine
    B. librium or tranxene
    C. valium or vistaril
    D. antiparkinson drugs

8. Which of the following is NOT true of extrapyramidal symptoms (EPS)? They

    A. may appear after many weeks of use of phenothiazines
    B. can safely be controlled without medical assistance
    C. may appear after the patient has been taking the drug for only a few days
    D. may include pseudoparkinsonism

9. The time required to reach an effective blood level for an antidepressant medication would MOST likely be three

    A. days   B. hours   C. weeks   D. months

10. An example of a psychotropic drug would be

    A. seconal   B. aspirin   C. librium   D. perichloz

11. In evaluating a patient you are meeting for the first time, it would be best NOT to

    A. be as objective as possible
    B. question one's own motives and reactions when processing data during and after the meeting
    C. be extremely goal-oriented
    D. not allow any praise or criticism directed at you by the patient to influence your assessment

12. All of the following statements are true EXCEPT:

    A. People communicate non-verbally via their behavior and their body posture
    B. Non-verbal clues may be a better indication of a patient's true feelings than what the patient actually says
    C. A patient who is highly anxious is easier to evaluate than a patient who is relatively calm
    D. People should be judged objectively

13. When asking a patient a question, one should do all of the following EXCEPT

    A. phrase questions in order to receive a yes or no response
    B. ask only relevant questions
    C. listen carefully to the response before asking the next question
    D. phrase questions clearly

14. The MAIN purpose for extensive record keeping is to

    A. provide an accurate description of the patient's diagnosis
    B. provide a subjective report of the patient's behavior
    C. provide an objective report of the patient's behavior
    D. give mental health personnel something to do

15. When talking to a patient for the first time, one must realize that

    A. hostile behavior indicates an extremely severe disorder in the patient
    B. a patient's physical appearance will indicate how successful you will be in communicating with the patient
    C. the patient is extremely nervous
    D. you are both strangers to each other

16. Of the following, which statement is NOT true?

    A. The rapid assessment of a patient is not necessarily accomplished by asking a series of routine questions.
    B. There is value, in assessing a patient, in creating a conversational bridge which has *here and now* relevance.
    C. One can assess a patient's state by his or her reaction to a warm greeting given to him or her.
    D. There is some value in routinely asking certain questions, when needed, in order to check a patient's orientation and memory.

17. All of the following could be signs that someone is moving towards mental illness EXCEPT

    A. exhibiting a degree of prolonged, constant anxiety, apprehension, or fear which is out of proportion with reality
    B. severe appetite disturbances
    C. occasional depression
    D. abrupt changes in a person's behavior

18. The first few minutes of interaction with a patient can reveal all but

    A. a patient's contact with reality
    B. whether you are comfortable with a patient
    C. a patient's mood
    D. a patient's chances for recovery

19. Which of the following statements is TRUE?

    A. The tentative diagnosis made when a patient is first admitted is the most accurate diagnosis.
    B. One should always try and keep in mind the state the patient was in when first admitted.
    C. A diagnosis is actually an ongoing process.
    D. When assessing patients' behavior, it is best to be suspicious of what may look like progress.

20. All of the following are examples of defense mechanisms EXCEPT

    A. projection
    B. complimenting someone
    C. displacement
    D. regression

21. A treatment plan is likely to be MOST effective if the

    A. patient's suggestions are always incorporated
    B. patient is voluntarily and wholeheartedly participating in the treatment plan designed for him or her

C. patient has daily contact with his or her family
D. patient respects the team leader

22. All of the following are true EXCEPT:

    A. Patients do not become well simply by people doing something for them
    B. A patient's well-being is enhanced when one or more team members can forge a *therapeutic alliance* with that patient
    C. The most important purpose of the treatment team is to administer the proper medications to patients
    D. It is important that a patient be seen as an individual, and not just as a *case* or a *number*

22.____

23. Of the following, a member of the treatment team can BEST assist a patient by

    A. commanding respect from other team members
    B. carefully observing the behavior of patients
    C. avoiding spending too much time with patients
    D. becoming friends with a patient

23.____

24. Of the following, which is LEAST important when considering a treatment plan?

    A. Involving the patient
    B. Setting reasonable goals
    C. Being as specific as possible in setting completion dates for goals, and sticking to them
    D. Detailing the methods to be followed, and the work assignments

24.____

25. All of the following are true EXCEPT:

    A. A treatment team should help patients understand that they can improve their condition if they will cooperate with the treatment plan
    B. Patients should be encouraged to participate in the programs designed for them
    C. Patients should be encouraged to revise their treatment plans
    D. One's approach should be tailored for each individual, whenever possible

25.____

26. All of the following could be considered appropriate goals for patients to work towards, EXCEPT to

    A. expand one's capacity to find or create acceptable options
    B. learn to be less dependent
    C. give up feeling persecuted
    D. learn how to get what one needs, at any cost

26.____

27. In working in treatment teams, it is MOST important for team members to

    A. communicate effectively with each other
    B. enjoy working with each other
    C. keep morale high
    D. attend meetings on time

27.____

28. One of the purposes of the treatment team is to

    A. decrease the amount of work
    B. coordinate and integrate services to patients
    C. provide training
    D. provide patients with basic counseling skills they can use

29. When working with someone exhibiting a manic-depressive psychosis, depressed type, it is BEST to

    A. concern yourself primarily with his or her eating habits
    B. focus primarily on their sleeping habits
    C. take every statement he or she may make about suicide seriously
    D. allow them to watch a great deal of television

30. In working with a paranoid patient, all of the following are true EXCEPT: It

    A. is important to listen with respect
    B. is helpful to establish a trusting relationship
    C. is good to try and talk the patient out of his or her fears
    D. would not be a good practice to agree with their statements, if they are not true

31. It is important, when dealing with verbally abusive patients, to keep in mind all of the following EXCEPT:

    A. Patients usually become abusive because of frustrating circumstances beyond their control
    B. In most cases, the patients do not mean anything personal by their abusive remarks; they are displacing anger
    C. It is important for staff members to remain calm and controlled when patients have emotional outbursts
    D. It is a good idea to allow an angry patient to draw you into an argument, as this will eventually help calm him or her down

32. When dealing with a patient who insists upon doing a number of rituals before brushing his teeth, it would be BEST to

    A. attempt to tease him out of his behavior
    B. not be critical of the ritualistic behavior
    C. perform the same rituals so that he feels more secure
    D. insist that he eliminate one step of the ritual each week

33. A patient tells you that he is balancing an automobile on the top of his head, and asks you what you think of that.
    An APPROPRIATE response for you to make would be:

    A. to ask him to take you for a ride
    B. *Stop saying ridiculous things*
    C. *I know you believe you are balancing a car on your head but I don't see it, therefore I have to assume that you're not*
    D. *Is it an invisible car*

34. A new patient, who is very paranoid, refuses to take off his clothes before getting into bed.
    Which would be MOST helpful?

    A. Getting another staff member to assist in removing his clothes
    B. Leaving the room until he comes to his senses
    C. Trying to find out why the patient does not want to undress
    D. Allowing the patient to stay up all night

35. In handling depressed patients, it is BEST to

    A. encourage them to participate in activities
    B. remind them often that things will be better tomorrow
    C. remember that depressed patients have few feelings of guilt
    D. let them know that you know just how they are feeling

36. A patient tells you that she is very depressed over the recent death of her brother.
    Which of the following would be the MOST appropriate response?

    A. *Everybody gets depressed when they lose someone they love.*
    B. *It could have been worse; at least he was ill only a short time.*
    C. *I know just how you feel.*
    D. *This must be very difficult for you.*

37. A patient who recently suffered a stroke refuses to let you help her bathe.
    This is probably because

    A. it is hard for her to accept that she can no longer do things for herself that she could do before the stroke
    B. she does not like you
    C. she is extremely independent and should be encouraged to be less so
    D. you need to review your methods for bathing patients

38. All of the following would be appropriate in working with a patient who is hallucinating EXCEPT

    A. carefully watch what you are non-verbally communicating
    B. ask concrete, reality-oriented questions
    C. provide a calm, structured environment
    D. agree with the patient, if asked, that you are experiencing the same state he or she is

39. In dealing with overactive patients, it is BEST to

    A. not give most of your attention to these patients, leaving the quieter patients to look after themselves
    B. keep in mind that overactive patients are always more interesting than other patients
    C. remember that overactive patients need more care than other patients
    D. forcibly restrain them whenever possible

40. A patient with mild organic brain damage is very withdrawn and negativistic. 40.____
 The BEST approach, of the following, would be
    A. *I need a partner to play cards with me*
    B. *Your family is very disappointed in you when you act like this*
    C. *Your doctor said you should participate in all activities here, so you'd better do that*
    D. *Would you like to go to your room so you can be alone?*

KEY (CORRECT ANSWERS)

1.	C	11.	C	21.	B	31.	D
2.	A	12.	C	22.	C	32.	B
3.	D	13.	A	23.	B	33.	C
4.	C	14.	C	24.	C	34.	C
5.	B	15.	D	25.	C	35.	A
6.	C	16.	C	26.	D	36.	D
7.	A	17.	C	27.	A	37.	A
8.	B	18.	D	28.	B	38.	D
9.	C	19.	C	29.	C	39.	A
10.	C	20.	B	30.	C	40.	A

READING COMPREHENSION
UNDERSTANDING AND INTERPRETING WRITTEN MATERIAL
EXAMINATION SECTION
TEST 1

Questions 1-8.

DIRECTIONS: Each question or incomplete statement is followed by several suggested answers or completions. Select the one that BEST answers the question or completes the statement. *PRINT THE LETTER OF THE CORRECT ANSWER IN THE SPACE AT THE RIGHT.*

Questions 1 and 2.

DIRECTIONS: Your answers to Questions 1 and 2 must be based ONLY on the information given in the following paragraph.

Hospitals maintained wholly by public taxation may treat only those compensation cases which are emergencies and may not treat such emergency cases longer than the emergency exists; provided, however, that these restrictions shall not be applicable where there is not available a hospital other than a hospital maintained wholly by taxation.

1. According to the above paragraph, compensation cases

    A. are regarded as emergency cases by hospitals maintained wholly by public taxation
    B. are seldom treated by hospitals maintained wholly by public taxation
    C. are treated mainly by privately endowed hospitals
    D. may be treated by hospitals maintained wholly by public taxation if they are emergencies

    1.____

2. According to the above paragraph, it is MOST reasonable to conclude that where a privately endowed hospital is available,

    A. a hospital supported wholly by public taxation may treat emergency compensation cases only so long as the emergency exists
    B. a hospital supported wholly by public taxation may treat any compensation cases
    C. a hospital supported wholly by public taxation must refer emergency compensation cases to such a hospital
    D. the restrictions regarding the treatment of compensation cases by a tax-supported hospital are not wholly applicable

    2.____

Questions 3-7.

DIRECTIONS: Answer Questions 3 through 7 ONLY according to the information given in the following passage.

THE MANUFACTURE OF LAUNDRY SOAP

The manufacture of soap is not a complicated process. Soap is a fat or an oil, plus an alkali, water and salt. The alkali used in making commercial laundry soap is caustic soda. The salt used is the same as common table salt. A fat is generally an animal product that is not a liquid at room temperature. If heated, it becomes a liquid. An oil is generally liquid at room temperature. If the temperature is lowered, the oil becomes a solid just like ordinary fat.

At the soap plant, a huge tank five stories high, called a *kettle,* is first filled part way with fats and then the alkali and water are added. These ingredients are then heated and boiled together. Salt is then poured into the top of the boiling solution; and as the salt slowly sinks down through the mixture, it takes with it the glycerine which comes from the melted fats. The product which finally comes from the kettle is a clear soap which has a moisture content of about 34%. This clear soap is then chilled so that more moisture is driven out. As a result, the manufacturer finally ends up with a commercial laundry soap consisting of 88% clear soap and only 12% moisture.

3. An ingredient used in making laundry soap is

   A. table sugar
   B. potash
   C. glycerine
   D. caustic soda

4. According to the above passage, a difference between fats and oils is that fats

   A. cost more than oils
   B. are solid at room temperature
   C. have less water than oils
   D. are a liquid animal product

5. According to the above passage, the MAIN reason for using salt in the manufacture of soap is to

   A. make the ingredients boil together
   B. keep the fats in the kettle melted
   C. remove the glycerine
   D. prevent the loss of water from the soap

6. According to the passage, the purpose of chilling the clear soap is to

   A. stop the glycerine from melting
   B. separate the alkali from the fats
   C. make the oil become solid
   D. get rid of more moisture

7. According to the passage, the percentage of moisture in commercial laundry soap is

   A. 12%   B. 34%   C. 66%   D. 88%

8. The x-ray has gone into business. Developed primarily to aid in diagnosing human ills, the machine now works in packing plants, in foundries, in service stations, and in a dozen ways to contribute to precision and accuracy in industry.
   The above statement means *most nearly* that the x-ray

   A. was first developed to aid business
   B. is of more help to business than it is to medicine
   C. is being used to improve the functioning of business
   D. is more accurate for packing plants than it is for foundries

8.____

Questions 9-25.

DIRECTIONS: Each question consists of a statement. You are to indicate whether the statement is TRUE (T) or FALSE (F). *PRINT THE LETTER OF THE CORRECT ANSWER IN THE SPACE AT THE RIGHT.*

Questions 9-12.

DIRECTIONS: Read the paragraph below about *shock* and then answer Questions 9 through 12 according to the information given in the paragraph.

SHOCK

While not found in all injuries, shock is present in all serious injuries caused by accidents. During shock, the normal activities of the body slow down. This partly explains why one of the signs of shock is a pale, cold skin, since insufficient blood goes to the body parts during shock.

9. If the injury caused by an accident is serious, shock is sure to be present.   9.____

10. In shock, the heart beats faster than normal.   10.____

11. The face of a person suffering from shock is usually red and flushed.   11.____

12. Not enough blood goes to different parts of the body during shock.   12.____

Questions 13-18.

DIRECTIONS: Questions 13 through 18, inclusive, are to be answered SOLELY on the basis of the information contained in the following statement and NOT upon any other information you may have.

Blood transfusions are given to patients at the hospital upon recommendation of the physicians attending such cases. The physician fills out a *Request for Blood Transfusion* form in duplicate and sends both copies to the Medical Director's office, where a list is maintained of persons called *donors* who desire to sell their blood for transfusions. A suitable donor is selected, and the transfusion is given. Donors are, in many instances, medical students and employees of the hospital. Donors receive twenty-five dollars for each transfusion.

13. According to the above paragraph, a blood donor is paid twenty-five dollars for each transfusion.   13.____

14. According to the above paragraph, only medical students and employees of the hospital are selected as blood donors. 14.___

15. According to the above paragraph, the *Request for Blood Transfusion* form is filled out by the patient and sent to the Medical Director's office. 15.___

16. According to the above paragraph, a list of blood donors is maintained in the Medical Director's office. 16.___

17. According to the above paragraph, cases for which the attending physicians recommend blood transfusions are usually emergency cases. 17.___

18. According to the above paragraph, one copy of the *Request for Blood Transfusion* form is kept by the patient and one copy is sent to the Medical Director's office. 18.___

Questions 19-25.

DIRECTIONS: Questions 19 through 25, inclusive, are to be answered SOLELY on the basis of the information contained in the following passage and NOT upon any other information you may have.

Before being admitted to a hospital ward, a patient is first interviewed by the Admitting Clerk, who records the patient's name, age, sex, race, birthplace, and mother's maiden name. This clerk takes all of the money and valuables that the patient has on his person. A list of the valuables is written on the back of the envelope in which the valuables are afterwards placed. Cash is counted and placed in a separate envelope, and the amount of money and the name of the patient are written on the outside of the envelope. Both envelopes are sealed, fastened together, and placed in a compartment of a safe.

An orderly then escorts the patient to a dressing room where the patient's clothes are removed and placed in a bundle. A tag bearing the patient's name is fastened to the bundle. A list of the contents of the bundle is written on property slips, which are made out in triplicate. The information contained on the outside of the envelopes containing the cash and valuables belonging to the patient is also copied on the property slips.

According to the above passage,

19. patients are escorted to the dressing room by the Admitting Clerk. 19.___

20. the patient's cash and valuables are placed together in one envelope. 20.___

21. the number of identical property slips that are made out when a patient is being admitted to a hospital ward is three. 21.___

22. the full names of both parents of a patient are recorded by the Admitting Clerk before a patient is admitted to a hospital ward. 22.___

23. the amount of money that a patient has on his person when admitted to the hospital is entered on the patient's property slips. 23.___

24. an orderly takes all the money and valuables that a patient has on his person. 24.___

25. the patient's name is placed on the tag that is attached to the bundle containing the patient's clothing. 25.___

KEY (CORRECT ANSWERS)

1. D
2. A
3. D
4. B
5. C

6. D
7. A
8. C
9. T
10. F

11. F
12. T
13. T
14. F
15. F

16. T
17. T
18. F
19. F
20. F

21. T
22. F
23. T
24. F
25. T

TEST 2

DIRECTIONS: Each question or incomplete statement is followed by several suggested answers or completions. Select the one that BEST answers the question or completes the statement. *PRINT THE LETTER OF THE CORRECT ANSWER IN THE SPACE AT THE RIGHT.*

Questions 1-4.

DIRECTIONS: Questions 1 through 4 are to be answered in accordance with the following paragraphs.

One fundamental difference between the United States health care system and the health care systems of some European countries is the way that hospital charges for long-term illnesses affect their citizens.

In European countries such as England, Sweden, and Germany, citizens can face, without fear, hospital charges due to prolonged illness, no matter how substantial they may be. Citizens of these nations are required to pay nothing when they are hospitalized, for they have prepaid their treatment as taxpayers when they were well and were earning incomes.

On the other hand, the United States citizen, in spite of the growth of payments by third parties which include private insurance carriers as well as public resources, has still to shoulder 40 percent of hospital care costs, while his private insurance contributes only 25 percent and public resources the remaining 35 percent.

Despite expansion of private health insurance and social legislation in the United States, out-of-pocket payments for hospital care by individuals have steadily increased. Such payments, currently totalling $23 billion, are nearly twice as high as ten years ago.

Reform is inevitable and, when it comes, will have to reconcile sharply conflicting interests. Hospital staffs are demanding higher and higher wages. Hospitals are under pressure by citizens, who as patients demand more and better services but who as taxpayers or as subscribers to hospital insurance plans, are reluctant to pay the higher cost of improved care. An acceptable reconciliation of these interests has so far eluded legislators and health administrators in the United States.

1. According to the above passage, the one of the following which is an ADVANTAGE that citizens of England, Sweden, and Germany have over United States citizens is that, when faced with long-term illness,   1.___

    A. the amount of out-of-pocket payments made by these European citizens is small when compared to out-of-pocket payments made by United States citizens
    B. European citizens have no fear of hospital costs no matter how great they may be
    C. more efficient and reliable hospitals are available to the European citizen than is available to the United States citizens
    D. a greater range of specialized hospital care is available to the European citizens than is available to the United States citizens

2. According to the above passage, reform of the United States system of health care must reconcile all of the following EXCEPT

    A. attempts by health administrators to provide improved hospital care
    B. taxpayers' reluctance to pay for the cost of more and better hospital services
    C. demands by hospital personnel for higher wages
    D. insurance subscribers' reluctance to pay the higher costs of improved hospital care

2.____

3. According to the above passage, the out-of-pocket payments for hospital care that individuals made ten years ago was APPROXIMATELY _____ billion.

    A. $32   B. $23   C. $12   D. $3

3.____

4. According to the above passage, the GREATEST share of the costs of hospital care in the United States is paid by

    A. United States citizens
    B. private insurance carriers
    C. public resources
    D. third parties

4.____

Questions 5-8.

DIRECTIONS: Questions 5 through 8 are to be answered SOLELY on the basis of the information contained in the following passage.

Effective cost controls have been difficult to establish in most hospitals in the United States. Ways must be found to operate hospitals with reasonable efficiency without sacrificing quality and in a manner that will reduce the amount of personal income now being spent on health care and the enormous drain on national resources. We must adopt a new public objective of providing higher quality health care at significantly lower cost. One step that can be taken to achieve this goal is to carefully control capital expenditures for hospital construction and expansion. Perhaps the way to start is to declare a moratorium on all hospital construction and to determine the factors that should be considered in deciding whether a hospital should be built. Such factors might include population growth, distance to the nearest hospital, availability of medical personnel, and hospital bed shortage.

A second step to achieve the new objective is to increase the ratio of out-of-hospital patient to in-hospital patient care. This can be done by using separate health care facilities other than hospitals to attract patients who have increasingly been going to hospital clinics and overcrowding them. Patients should instead identify with a separate health care facility to keep them out of hospitals.

A third step is to require better hospital operating rules and controls. This step might include the review of a doctor's performance by other doctors, outside professional evaluations of medical practice, and required refresher courses and re-examinations for doctors. Other measures might include obtaining mandatory second opinions on the need for surgery in order to avoid unnecessary surgery, and outside review of work rules and procedures to eliminate unnecessary testing of patients.

A fourth step is to halt the construction and public subsidizing of new medical schools and to fill whatever needs exist in professional coverage by emphasizing the medical training of physicians with specialities that are in short supply and by providing a better geographic distribution of physicians and surgeons.

5. According to the above passage, providing higher quality health care at lower cost can be achieved by the

   A. greater use of out-of-hospital facilities
   B. application of more effective cost controls on doctors' fees
   C. expansion of improved in-hospital patient care services at hospital clinics
   D. development of more effective training programs in hospital administration

6. According to the above passage, the one of the following which should be taken into account in determining if a hospital should be constructed is the

   A. number of out-of-hospital health care facilities
   B. availability of public funds to subsidize construction
   C. number of hospitals under construction
   D. availability of medical personnel

7. According to the above passage, it is IMPORTANT to operate hospitals efficiently because

   A. they are currently in serious financial difficulties
   B. of the need to reduce the amount of personal income going to health care
   C. the quality of health care services has deteriorated
   D. of the need to increase productivity goals to take care of the growing population in the United States

8. According to the above passage, which one of the following approaches is MOST LIKELY to result in better operating rules and controls in hospitals?

   A. Allocating doctors to health care facilities on the basis of patient population
   B. Equalizing the workloads of doctors
   C. Establishing a physician review board to evaluate the performance of other physicians
   D. Eliminating unnecessary outside review of patient testing

Questions 9-14.

DIRECTIONS: Questions 9 through 14 are to be answered SOLELY on the basis of the information contained in the following passage.

The United States today is the only major industrial nation in the world without a system of national health insurance or a national health service. Instead, we have placed our prime reliance on private enterprise and private health insurance to meet the need. Yet, in a recent year, of the 180 million Americans under 65 years of age, 34 million had no hospital insurance, 38 million had no surgical insurance, 63 million had no out-patient x-ray and laboratory insurance, 94 million had no insurance for prescription drugs, and 103 million had no insurance for physician office visits or home visits. Some 35 million Americans under the age of 65 had no health insurance whatsoever. Some 64 million additional Americans under age 65 had health insurance coverage that was less than that provided to the aged under Medicare.

Despite more than three decades of enormous growth, the private health insurance industry today pays benefits equal to only one-third of the total cost of private health care, leaving the rest to be borne by the patient—essentially the same ratio which held true a decade ago. Moreover, nearly all private health insurance is limited; it provides partial benefits, not comprehensive benefits; acute care, not preventive care; it siphons off the young and healthy, and ignores the poor and medically indigent. The typical private carrier usually pays only the cost of hospital care, forcing physicians and patients alike to resort to wasteful and inefficient use of hospital facilities, thereby giving further impetus to the already soaring costs of hospital care. Valuable hospital beds are used for routine tests and examinations. Unnecessary hospitalization, unnecessary surgery, and unnecessarily extended hospital stays are encouraged. These problems are exacerbated by the fact that administrative costs of commercial carriers are substantially higher than they are for Blue Shield, Blue Cross, or Medicare.

9. According to the above passage, the PROPORTION of total private health care costs paid by private health insurance companies today as compared to ten years ago has

   A. *increased* by approximately one-third
   B. *remained* practically the same
   C. *increased* by approximately two-thirds
   D. *decreased* by approximately one-third

10. According to the above passage, the one of the following which has contributed MOST to wasteful use of hospital facilities is the

    A. increased emphasis on preventive health care
    B. practice of private carriers of providing comprehensive health care benefits
    C. increased hospitalization of the elderly and the poor
    D. practice of a number of private carriers of paying only for hospital care costs

11. Based on the information in the above passage, which one of the following patients would be LEAST likely to receive benefits from a typical private health insurance plan?
    A

    A. young patient who must undergo an emergency appendectomy
    B. middle-aged patient who needs a costly series of x-ray and laboratory tests for diagnosis of gastrointestinal complaints
    C. young patient who must visit his physician weekly for treatment of a chronic skin disease
    D. middle-aged patient who requires extensive cancer surgery

12. Which one of the following is the MOST accurate inference that can be drawn from the above passage?

    A. Private health insurance has failed to fully meet the health care needs of Americans.
    B. Most Americans under age 65 have health insurance coverage better than that provided to the elderly under Medicare.
    C. Countries with a national health service are likely to provide poorer health care for their citizens than do countries that rely primarily on private health insurance.
    D. Hospital facilities in the United States are inadequate to meet the nation's health care needs.

13. Of the total number of Americans under age 65, what percentage belonged in the combined category of persons with NO health insurance or health insurance less than that provided to the aged under Medicare?

    A. 19% B. 36% C. 55% D. 65%

14. According to the above passage, the one of the following types of health insurance which covered the SMALLEST number of Americans under age 65 was

    A. hospital insurance
    B. surgical insurance
    C. insurance for prescription drugs
    D. insurance for physician office or home visits

Questions 15-17.

DIRECTIONS: Questions 15 through 17 are to be answered SOLELY on the basis of the information contained in the following passage.

Statistical studies have demonstrated that disease and mortality rates are higher among the poor than among the more affluent members of our society. Periodic surveys conducted by the United States Public Health Service continue to document a higher prevalence of infectious and chronic diseases within low income families. While the basic life style and living conditions of the poor are to a considerable extent responsible for this less favorable health status, there are indications that the kind of health care received by the poor also plays a significant role. The poor are less likely to be aware of the concepts and practices of scientific medicine and less likely to seek health care when they need it. Moreover, they are discouraged from seeking adequate health care by the depersonalization, disorganization, and inadequate emphasis on preventive care which characterize the health care most often provided for them.

To achieve the objective of better health care for the poor, the following approaches have been suggested: encouraging the poor to seek preventive care as well as care for acute illness and to establish a lasting one-to-one relationship with a single physician who can treat the poor patient as a whole individual; sufficient financial subsidy to put the poor on an equal footing with *paying patients,* thereby giving them the opportunity to choose from among available health services providers; inducements to health services providers to establish public clinics in poverty areas; and legislation to provide for health education, earlier detection of disease, and coordinated health care.

15. According to the above passage, the one of the following which is a function of the United States Public Health Service is

    A. gathering data on the incidence of infectious diseases
    B. operating public health clinics in poverty areas lacking private physicians
    C. recommending legislation for the improvement of health care in the United States
    D. encouraging the poor to participate in programs aimed at the prevention of illness

16. According to the above passage, the one of the following which is MOST characteristic of the health care currently provided for the poor is that it

    A. aims at establishing clinics in poverty areas
    B. enables the poor to select the health care they want through the use of financial subsidies
    C. places insufficient stress on preventive health care
    D. over-emphasizes the establishment of a one-to-one relationship between physician and patient

17. The above passage IMPLIES that the poor lack the financial resources to

    A. obtain adequate health insurance coverage
    B. select from among existing health services
    C. participate in health education programs
    D. lobby for legislation aimed at improving their health care

Questions 18-20.

DIRECTIONS: Questions 18 through 20 are to be answered SOLELY on the basis of the information contained in the following passage.

The concept of *affiliation,* developed more than ten years ago, grew out of a series of studies which found evidence of faulty care, surgery of *questionable* value and other undesirable conditions in the city's municipal hospitals. The affiliation agreements signed shortly thereafter were designed to correct these deficiencies by assuring high quality medical care. In general, the agreements provided the staff and expertise of a voluntary hospital—sometimes connected with a medical school—to operate various services or, in some cases, all of the professional divisions of a specific municipal hospital. The municipal hospitals have paid for these services, which last year cost the city $200 million, the largest single expenditure of the Health and Hospitals Corporation. In addition, the municipal hospitals have provided to the voluntary hospitals such facilities as free space for laboratories and research. While some experts agree that affiliation has resulted in improvements in some hospital care, they contend that many conditions that affiliation was meant to correct still exist. In addition, accountability procedures between the Corporation and voluntary hospitals are said to be so inadequate that audits of affiliation contracts of the past five years revealed that there may be more than $200 million in charges for services by the voluntary hospitals which have not been fully substantiated. Consequently, the Corporation has proposed that future agreements provide accountability in terms of funds, services supplied, and use of facilities by the voluntary hospitals.

18. According to the above passage, *affiliation* may BEST be defined as an agreement whereby

    A. voluntary hospitals pay for the use of municipal hospital facilities
    B. voluntary and municipal hospitals work to eliminate duplication of services
    C. municipal hospitals pay voluntary hospitals for services performed
    D. voluntary and municipal hospitals transfer patients to take advantage of specialized services

19. According to the above passage, the MAIN purpose for setting up the *affiliation* agreement was to

    A. supplement the revenues of municipal hospitals
    B. improve the quality of medical care in municipal hospitals
    C. reduce operating costs in municipal hospitals
    D. increase the amount of space available to municipal hospitals

20. According to the above passage, inadequate accountability procedures have resulted in

    A. unsubstantiated charges for services by the voluntary hospitals
    B. emphasis on research rather than on patient care in municipal hospitals
    C. unsubstantiated charges for services by the municipal hospitals
    D. economic losses to voluntary hospitals

Questions 21-25.

DIRECTIONS: Questions 21 through 25 are to be answered SOLELY on the basis of the information contained in the following passage.

The payment for medical services covered under the Outpatient Medical Insurance Plan (OMI) may be made, by OMI, directly to a physician or to the OMI patient. If the physician and the patient agree that the physician is to receive payment directly from OMI, the payment will be officially assigned to the physician; this is the assignment method. If payment is not assigned, the patient receives payment directly from OMI based on an itemized bill he submits, regardless of whether or not he has already paid his physician.

When a physician accepts assignment of the payment for medical services, he agrees that total charges will not be more than the allowed charge determined by the OMI carrier administering the program. In such cases, the OMI patient pays any unmet part of the $85 annual deductible, plus 10 percent of the remaining charges to the physician. In unassigned claims, the patient is responsible for the total amount charged by the physician. The patient will then be reimbursed by the program 90 percent of the allowed charges in excess of the annual deductible.

The rates of acceptance of assignments provide a measure of how many OMI patients are spared *administrative participation* in the program. Because physicians are free to accept or reject assignments, the rate in which assignments are made provide a general indication of the medical community's satisfaction with the OMI program, especially with the level of amounts paid by the program for specific services and the promptness of payment.

21. According to the above passage, in order for a physician to receive payment directly from OMI for medical services to an OMI patient, the physician would have to accept the assignment of payment, to have the consent of the patient, AND to

    A. submit to OMI a paid itemized bill
    B. collect from the patient 90% of the total bill
    C. collect from the patient the total amount of the charges for his services, a portion of which he will later reimburse the patient
    D. agree that his charges for services to the patient will not exceed the amount allowed by the program

22. According to the above passage, if a physician accepts assignment of payment, the patient pays   22.____

    A. the total amount charged by the physician and is reimbursed by the program for 90 percent of the allowed charges in excess of the applicable deductible
    B. any unmet part of the $85 annual deductible, plus 90 percent of the remaining charges
    C. the total amount charged by the physician and is reimbursed by the program for 10 percent of the allowed charges in excess of the $85 annual deductible
    D. any unmet part of the $85 annual deductible, plus 10 percent of the remaining charges

23. A physician has accepted the assignment of payment for charges to an OMI patient. The physician's charges, all of which are allowed under OMI, amount to $115. This is the first time the patient has been eligible for OMI benefits and the first time the patient has received services from this physician.   23.____
    According to the above passage, the patient must pay the physician

    A. $27   B. $76.50   C. $88   D. $103.50

24. In an unassigned claim, a physician's charges, all of which are allowed under OMI, amount to $165. The patient paid the physician the full amount of the bill.   24.____
    If this is the FIRST time the patient has been eligible for OMI benefits, he will receive from OMI a reimbursement of

    A. $72   B. $80   C. $85   D. $93

25. According to the above passage, if the rate of acceptance of assignments by physicians is high, it is LEAST appropriate to conclude that the medical community is generally satisfied with the   25.____

    A. supplementary medical insurance program
    B. levels of amounts paid to physicians by the program
    C. number of OMI patients being spared administrative participation in the program
    D. promptness of the program in making payment for services

KEY (CORRECT ANSWERS)

1. B	11. C	21. D
2. A	12. A	22. D
3. C	13. C	23. C
4. D	14. D	24. A
5. A	15. A	25. C
6. D	16. C	
7. B	17. B	
8. C	18. C	
9. B	19. B	
10. D	20. A	

PREPARING WRITTEN MATERIAL
EXAMINATION SECTION
TEST 1

DIRECTIONS: Each question consists of a sentence which may or may not be an example of good English usage. Examine each sentence, considering grammar, punctuation, spelling, capitalization, and awkwardness. Then choose the correct statement about it from the four choices below it. If the English usage in the sentence given is better than any of the changes suggested in choices B, C, or D, pick choice A. (Do not pick a choice that will change the meaning of the sentence.) *PRINT THE LETTER OF THE CORRECT ANSWER IN THE SPACE AT THE RIGHT.*

1. We attended a staff conference on Wednesday the new safety and fire rules were discussed.   1._____
    A. This is an example of acceptable writing.
    B. The words "safety," "fire," and "rules" should begin with capital letters.
    C. There should be a comma after the word "Wednesday."
    D. There should be a period after the word "Wednesday" and the word "the" should begin with a capital letter.

2. Neither the dictionary or the telephone directory could be found in the office library.   2._____
    A. This is an example of acceptable writing.
    B. The word "or" should be changed to "nor."
    C. The word "library" should be spelled "libery."
    D. The word "neither" should be changed to "either."

3. The report would have been typed correctly if the typist could read the draft.   3._____
    A. This is an example of acceptable writing.
    B. The word "would" should be removed.
    C. The word "have" should be inserted after the word "could."
    D. The word "correctly" should be changed to "correct."

4. The supervisor brought the reports and forms to an employees desk.   4._____
    A. This is an example of acceptable writing.
    B. The word "brought" should be changed to "took."
    C. There should be a comma after the word "reports" and a comma after the word "forms."
    D. The word "employees" should be spelled "employee's."

5. It's important for all the office personnel to submit their vacation schedules on time.   5._____
    A. This is an example of acceptable writing.
    B. The word "It's" should be spelled "Its."
    C. The word "their" should be spelled "they're."
    D. The word "personnel" should be spelled "personal."

127

6. The report, along with the accompanying documents, were submitted for review. 6.____
   A. This is an example of acceptable writing.
   B. The words "were submitted" should be changed to "was submitted."
   C. The word "accompanying" should be spelled "accompaning."
   D. The comma after the word "report" should be taken out.

7. If others must use your files, be certain that they understand how the system works, but insist that you do all the filing and refiling. 7.____
   A. This is an example of acceptable writing.
   B. There should be a period after the word "works," and the word "but" should start a new sentence.
   C. The words "filing" and "refiling" should be spelled "fileing" and "refileing."
   D. There should be a comma after the word "but."

8. The appeal was not considered because of its late arrival. 8.____
   A. This is an example of acceptable writing.
   B. The word "its" should be changed to "it's."
   C. The word "its" should be changed to "the."
   D. The words "late arrival" should be changed to "arrival late."

9. The letter must be read carefuly to determine under which subject it should be filed. 9.____
   A. This is an example of acceptable writing.
   B. The word "under" should be changed to "at."
   C. The word "determine" should be spelled "determin."
   D. The word "carefuly" should be spelled "carefully."

10. He showed potential as an office manager, but he lacked skill in delegating work. 10.____
    A. This is an example of acceptable writing.
    B. The word "delegating" should be spelled "delagating."
    C. The word "potential" should be spelled "potencial."
    D. The words "he lacked" should be changed to "was lacking."

KEY (CORRECT ANSWERS)

1. D   6. B
2. B   7. A
3. C   8. A
4. D   9. D
5. A   10. A

TEST 2

DIRECTIONS: Each question consists of a sentence which may or may not be an example of good English usage. Examine each sentence, considering grammar, punctuation, spelling, capitalization, and awkwardness. Then choose the correct statement about it from the four choices below it. If the English usage in the sentence given is better than any of the changes suggested in choices B, C, or D, pick choice A. (Do not pick a choice that will change the meaning of the sentence.) *PRINT THE LETTER OF THE CORRECT ANSWER IN THE SPACE AT THE RIGHT.*

1. The supervisor wants that all staff members report to the office at 9:00 A.M.
   A. This is an example of acceptable writing.
   B. The word "that" should be removed and the word "to" should be inserted after the word "members."
   C. There should be a comma after the word "wants" and a comma after the word "office."
   D. The word "wants" should be changed to "want" and the word "shall" should be inserted after the word "members."

2. Every morning the clerk opens the office mail and distributes it.
   A. This is an example of acceptable writing.
   B. The word "opens" should be changed to "open."
   C. The word "mail" should be changed to "letters."
   D. The word "it" should be changed to "them."

3. The secretary typed more fast on a desktop computer than on a laptop computer.
   A. This is an example of acceptable writing.
   B. The words "more fast" should be changed to "faster."
   C. There should be a comma after the words "desktop computer."
   D. The word "than" should be changed to "then."

4. The new stenographer needed a desk a computer, a chair and a blotter.
   A. This is an example of acceptable writing.
   B. The word "blotter" should be spelled "blodder."
   C. The word "stenographer" should begin with a capital letter.
   D. There should be a comma after the word "desk."

5. The recruiting officer said, "There are many different goverment jobs available."
   A. This is an example of acceptable writing.
   B. The word "There" should not be capitalized.
   C. The word "government" should be spelled "government."
   D. The comma after the word "said" should be removed.

6. He can recommend a mechanic whose work is reliable.
   A. This is an example of acceptable writing.
   B. The word "reliable" should be spelled "relyable."
   C. The word "whose" should be spelled "who's."
   D. The word "mechanic should be spelled "mecanic."

7. She typed quickly; like someone who had not a moment to lose. 7.____
    A. This is an example of acceptable writing.
    B. The word "not" should be removed.
    C. The semicolon should be changed to a comma.
    D. The word "quickly" should be placed before instead of after the word "typed."

8. She insisted that she had to much work to do. 8.____
    A. This is an example of acceptable writing.
    B. The word "insisted" should be spelled "incisted."
    C. The word "to" used in front of "much" should be spelled "too."
    D. The word "do" should be changed to "be done."

9. He excepted praise from his supervisor for a job well done. 9.____
    A. This is an example of acceptable writing.
    B. The word "excepted" should be spelled "accepted."
    C. The order of the words "well done" should be changed to "done well."
    D. There should be a comma after the word "supervisor."

10. What appears to be intentional errors in grammar occur several times in the passage. 10.____
    A. This is an example of acceptable writing.
    B. The word "occur" should be spelled "occurr."
    C. The word "appears" should be changed to "appear."
    D. The phrase "several times" should be changed to "from time to time."

KEY (CORRECT ANSWERS)

1.	B	6.	A
2.	A	7.	C
3.	B	8.	C
4.	D	9.	B
5.	C	10.	C

TEST 3

DIRECTIONS: Each question consists of a sentence which may or may not be an example of good English usage. Examine each sentence, considering grammar, punctuation, spelling, capitalization, and awkwardness. Then choose the correct statement about it from the four choices below it. If the English usage in the sentence given is better than any of the changes suggested in choices B, C, or D, pick choice A. (Do not pick a choice that will change the meaning of the sentence.) *PRINT THE LETTER OF THE CORRECT ANSWER IN THE SPACE AT THE RIGHT.*

1. The clerk could have completed the assignment on time if he knows where these materials were located.
    A. This is an example of acceptable writing.
    B. The word "knows" should be replaced by "had known."
    C. The word "were" should be replaced by "had been."
    D. The words "where these materials were located" should be replaced by "the location of these materials."

2. All employees should be given safety training. Not just those who accidents.
    A. This is an example of acceptable writing.
    B. The period after the word "training" should be changed to a colon.
    C. The period after the word "training" should be changed to a semicolon, and the first letter of the word "Not" should be changed to a small "n."
    D. The period after the word "training" should be changed to a comma, and the first letter of the word "Not" should be changed to a small "n."

3. This proposal is designed to promote employee awareness of the suggestion program, to encourage employee participation in the program, and to increase the number of suggestions submitted.
    A. This is an example of acceptable writing.
    B. The word "proposal" should be spelled "proposal."
    C. The words "to increase the number of suggestions submitted" should be changed to "an increase in the number of suggestions is expected."
    D. The word "promote" should be changed to "enhance" and the word "increase" should be changed to "add to."

4. The introduction of inovative managerial techniques should be preceded by careful analysis of the specific circumstances and conditions in each department.
    A. This is an example of acceptable writing.
    B. The word "technique" should be spelled "techneques."
    C. The word "inovative" should be spelled "innovative."
    D. A comma should be placed after the word "circumstances" and after the word "conditions."

5. This occurrence indicates that such criticism embarrasses him. 5._____
   A. This is an example of acceptable writing.
   B. The word "occurrence" should be spelled "occurence."
   C. The word "criticism" should be spelled "critisism."
   D. The word "embarrasses" should be spelled "embarasses."

KEY (CORRECT ANSWERS)

1. B
2. D
3. A
4. C
5. A

PREPARING WRITTEN MATERIAL
EXAMINATION SECTION
TEST 1

DIRECTIONS: Each of the following sentences may be classified under one of the following four categories:
A. *Faulty* because of incorrect grammar or usage
B. *Faulty* because of incorrect punctuation or spelling
C. *Faulty* because of incorrect capitalization
D. *Correct*

Examine each sentence carefully. Then, in the correspondingly numbered space on the right, print the capital letter preceding the option which is the best of the four suggested above.

(All incorrect sentences contain but one type of error. Consider a sentence correct if it contains none of the types of errors mentioned, even though there may be other correct ways of expressing the same thought.

1. They gave the poor man some food when he approached. 1._____
2. I regret the loss caused by the error. 2._____
3. The students have a new teacher for shop mantenance. 3._____
4. They sweared to bring out all the facts. 4._____
5. He decided to open a branch store on 33rd street. 5._____
6. His speed is equal and more than that of a racehorse. 6._____
7. He felt very warm on that Summer day. 7._____
8. He was assisted by his friend, who lives in the next house. 8._____
9. The climate of New York is colder than California. 9._____
10. I shall wait for you on the corner. 10._____
11. Did we see the boy whose the leader? 11._____
12. Being a modest person, John seldom takes about his invention. 12._____
13. The gang is called the smith street boys. 13._____
14. He seen the man break into the store. 14._____

133

2 (#1)

15. We expected to lay still there for quite a while.   15.____
16. He is considered to be the Leader of his organization.   16.____
17. Although He received an invitation, He won't go.   17.____
18. The letter must be here some place.   18.____
19. I thought it to be he.   19.____
20. We expect to remain here for a long time.   20.____
21. The committee was agreed.   21.____
22. Two-thirds of the building are finished.   22.____
23. The water was froze.   23.____
24. Everyone of the salesmen must supply their own car.   24.____
25. Who is the author of Gone With the Wind?   25.____
26. He marched on and declaring that he would never surrender.   26.____
27. Who shall I say called?   27.____
28. Everyone has left but they.   28.____
29. Who did we give the order to?   29.____
30. Send your order in immediately.   30.____
31. I believe I paid the Bill.   31.____
32. I have not met but one person.   32.____
33. Why aren't Tom, and Fred, going to the dance?   33.____
34. What reason is there for him not going?   34.____
35. The seige of Malta was a tremendous event.   35.____
36. I was there yesterday I assure you.   36.____
37. Your ukulele is better than mine.   37.____
38. No one was there only Mary.   38.____

3 (#1)

39. The Capital city of Vermont is Montpelier.   39.____

40. Reggie Jackson may hit the largest amount of home runs this season.   40.____

KEY (CORRECT ANSWERS)

1.	B	11.	B	21.	D	31.	C
2.	D	12.	D	22.	A	32.	A
3.	B	13.	C	23.	A	33.	B
4.	A	14.	A	24.	A	34.	A
5.	C	15.	A	25.	B	35.	B
6.	A	16.	C	26.	A	36.	B
7.	C	17.	C	27.	D	37.	B
8.	D	18.	A	28.	D	38.	A
9.	A	19.	A	29.	A	39.	C
10.	D	20.	D	30.	D	40.	A

TEST 2

Questions 1-3.

DIRECTIONS: Questions 1 through 3 each consist of four sentences. Choose the one sentence in each set of four that would be BEST for a formal letter or report. Consider grammar and appropriate usage.

1. A. Most all the work he completed before he become ill.
   B. He completed most of the work before becoming ill.
   C. Prior to him becoming ill his work was mostly completed.
   D. Before he became will most of the work he had completed.

1.____

2. A. Being that the report lacked a clearly worded recommendation, it did not matter that it contained enough information.
   B. There was enough information in the report, although it, including the recommendation, were not clearly worded.
   C. Although the report contained enough information, it did not have a clearly worded recommendation.
   D. Though the report did not have a recommendation that was clearly worded, and the information therein contained was enough.

2.____

3. A. Having already overlooked the important mistakes, the ones which she found were not as important toward the end of the letter.
   B. Toward the end of the letter she had already overlooked the important mistakes, so that which she had found were not important.
   C. The mistakes which she had already overlooked were not as important as those which near the end of letter she had found.
   D. The mistakes which she found near the end of the letter were not so important as those which she had already overlooked.

3.____

Questions 4-5.

DIRECTIONS: Select the correct answer.

4. The unit has exceeded _____ goals and the employees are satisfied with _____ accomplishments.
   A. their; it's   B. it's, it's   C. is, there   D. its, their

4.____

5. Research indicates that employees who _____ no opportunity for close social relationships often find their work unsatisfying, and this _____ of satisfaction often reflects itself in low production.
   A. have, lack   B. have, excess   C. has, lack   D. has, excess

5.____

KEY (CORRECT ANSWERS)

1. B
2. C
3. D
4. D
5. A

TEST 3

DIRECTIONS: Select the choice which BEST expresses the thought and which contains NO errors in grammar or sentence construction.

1. A. She, hearing a signal, the source lamp flashed.
   B. While hearing a signal, the source lamp flashed
   C. In hearing a signal, the source lamp flashed.
   D. As she heard a signal, the source lamp flashed.

2. A. Every one of the time records have been initialed in the designated spaces.
   B. All of the time records has been initialed in the designated spaces.
   C. Which one of the time records was initialed in the designated spaces.
   D. The time records all been initialed in the designated spaces.

3. A. If there is no one else to answer the phone, you will have to answer it.
   B. You will have to answer it yourself if no one else answers the phone.
   C. If no one else is not around to pick up the phone, you have to do it.
   D. You will have to answer the phone when nobodys here to do it.

4. A. Dr. Byrnes not in his office. What could I do for you?
   B. Dr. Byrnes is not in his office. Is there something I can do for you?
   C. Since Dr. Byrnes is not in his office, might there be something I may do for you?
   D. Is there any ways I can assist you since Dr. Brynes is not in his office?

5. A. She do not understand how the new console works.
   B. The way the new console works, she doesn't understand.
   C. She doesn't understand how the new console works.
   D. The new console works, so that she doesn't understand.

KEY (CORRECT ANSWERS)

1. D
2. C
3. A
4. B
5. C

TEST 4

DIRECTIONS: The following questions each consist of a sentence which may or may not be an example of good English usage.

Consider grammar, punctuation, spelling, capitalization, awkwardness, etc.

Examine each sentence and then choose the correct statement about it from the four choices below. If the English usage in the sentence given is better than any of the changes suggested in options B, C, or D, choose option A. (Do not choose an option that will change the meaning of the sentence.)

1. The typist used an extention cord in order to connect her typewriter to the outlet nearest to her desk.
   A. This is an example of acceptable writing.
   B. A period should be placed after the word "cord" and the word "in" should have a capital "I."
   C. A comma should be placed after the word "typewriter."
   D. The word "extention" should be spelled "extension."

2. He would have went to the conference if he had received an invitation.
   A. This is an example of acceptable writing.
   B. The word "went" should be replaced by the word "gone."
   C. The word "had" should be replaced by "would have."
   D. The word "conference" should be spelled "conference."

3. In order to make the report neater, he spent many hours rewriting it.
   A. This is an example of acceptable writing.
   B. The word "more" should be inserted before the word "neater."
   C. There should be a colon after the word "neater."
   D. The word "spent" should be changed to "have spent."

4. His supervisor told him that he should of read the memorandum more carefully.
   A. This is an example of acceptable writing.
   B. The word "memorandum" should be spelled "memorandom."
   C. The word "of" should be replaced by the word "have."
   D. The word "carefully" should be replaced by the word "have."

5. It was decided that two separate reports should be written.
   A. This is an example of acceptable writing.
   B. A comma should be inserted after the word "decided."
   C. The word "be" should be replaced by the word "been."
   D. A colon should be inserted after the word "that."

6. She don't seem to understand that the work must be done as soon as possible.
   A. This is an example of acceptable writing.
   B. The word "doesn't" should replace the word "don't."
   C. The word "why" should replace the word "that."
   D. The word "as" before the word "soon" should be eliminated.

KEY (CORRECT ANSWERS)

1. D
2. B
3. A
4. C
5. A
6. B

PREPARING WRITTEN MATERIAL

PARAGRAPH REARRANGEMENT
COMMENTARY

The sentences that follow are in scrambled order. You are to rearrange them in proper order and indicate the letter choice containing the correct answer at the space at the right.

Each group of sentences in this section is actually a paragraph presented in scrambled order. Each sentence in the group has a place in that paragraph; no sentence is to be left out. You are to read each group of sentences and decide upon the best order in which to put the sentences so as to form a well-organized paragraph.

The questions in this section measure the ability to solve a problem when all the facts relevant to its solution are not given.

More specifically, certain positions of responsibility and authority require the employee to discover connection between events sometimes, apparently, unrelated. In order to do this, the employee will find it necessary to correctly infer that unspecified events have probably occurred or are likely to occur. This ability becomes especially important when action must be taken on incomplete information.

Accordingly, these questions require competitors to choose among several suggested alternatives, each of which presents a different sequential arrangement of the events. Competitors must choose the MOST logical of the suggested sequences.

In order to do so, they may be required to draw on general knowledge to infer missing concepts or events that are essential to sequencing the given events. Competitors should be careful to infer only what is essential to the sequence. The plausibility of the wrong alternatives will always require the inclusion of unlikely events or of additional chains of events which are NOT essential to sequencing the given events.

It's very important to remember that you are looking for the best of the four possible choices, and that the best choice of all may not even be one of the answers you're given to choose from.

There is no one right way to solve these problems. Many people have found it helpful to first write out the order of the sentences, as they would have arranged them, on their scrap paper before looking at the possible answers. If their optimum answer is there, this can save them some time. If it isn't, this method can still give insight into solving the problem. Others find it most helpful to just go through each of the possible choices, contrasting each as they go along. You should use whatever method feels comfortable and works for you.

While most of these types of questions are not that difficult, we've added a higher percentage of the difficult type, just to give you more practice. Usually there are only one or two questions on this section that contain such subtle distinctions that you're unable to answer confidently. And you then may find yourself stuck deciding between two possible choices, neither of which you're sure about.

EXAMINATION SECTION

TEST 1

DIRECTIONS: The sentences that follow are in scrambled order. You are to rearrange them in proper order and indicate the letter choice containing the correct answer. *PRINT THE LETTER OF THE CORRECT ANSWER IN THE SPACE AT THE RIGHT.*

1. Below are four statements labeled W, X, Y and Z. 1.____
   W. He was a strict and fanatic drillmaster.
   X. The word is always used in a derogatory sense and generally shows resentment and anger on the part of the user.
   Y. It is from the name of this Frenchman that we derive our English word, martinet.
   Z. Jean Martinet was the Inspector-General of Infantry during the reign of King Louis XIV.
   The PROPER order in which these sentences should be placed in a paragraph is:
   A. X, Z, W, Y   B. X, Z, Y, W   C. Z, W, Y, X   D. Z, Y, W, X

2. In the following paragraph, the sentences, which are numbered, have been jumbled. 2.____
   I. Since then it has undergone changes.
   II. It was incorporated in 1955 under the laws of the State of New York.
   III. Its primary purposes, a cleaner city, has, however, remained the same.
   IV. The Citizens Committee works in cooperation with the Mayor's Inter-departmental Committee for a Clean City. 3.____
   The order in which these sentences should be arranged to form a well-organized paragraph is:
   A. II, IV, I, III   B. III, IV, I, II   C. IV, II, I, III   D. IV, III, II, I

Questions 3-5.

DIRECTIONS: The sentences listed below are part of a meaningful paragraph but they are not given in their proper order. You are to decide what would be the BEST order in which to put the sentences so as to form a well-organized paragraph. Each sentence has a place in the paragraph; there are no extra sentences. You are then to answer Questions 3 through 5 inclusive on the basis of your rearrangements of these scrambled sentences into a properly organized paragraph.

In 1887 some insurance companies organized an Inspection Department to advise their clients on all phases of fire prevention and protection. Probably this has been due to the smaller annual fire losses in Great Britain than in the United States. It tests various fire prevention devices and appliances and determines manufacturing hazards and their safeguards. Fire research began earlier in the United States and is more advanced than in Great Britain. Later they established a laboratory specializing in electrical, mechanical, hydraulic, and chemical fields.

3. When the five sentences are arranged in proper order, the paragraph starts with the sentence which begins
   A. "In 1887..."   B. "Probably this..."   C. "It tests..."
   D. "Fire research..."   E. "Later they..."

4. In the last sentence listed above, "they" refers to
   A. the insurance companies   B. the United States and Great Britain
   C. the Inspection Department   D. clients
   E. technicians

5. When the above paragraph is properly arranged, it ends with the words
   A. "...and protection."   B. "...the United States."
   C. "...their safeguards."   D. "...in Great Britain."
   E. "...chemical fields."

KEY (CORRECT ANSWERS)

1. C
2. C
3. D
4. A
5. C

TEST 2

DIRECTIONS: In each of the questions numbered I through V, several sentences are given. For each question, choose as your answer the group of number that represents the MOST logical order of these sentences if they were arranged in paragraph form. *PRINT THE LETTER OF THE CORRECT ANSWER IN THE SPACE AT THE RIGHT.*

1. I. It is established when one shows that the landlord has prevented the tenant's enjoyment of his interest in the property leased.
    II. Constructive eviction is the result of a breach of the covenant of quiet enjoyment implied in all leases.
    III. In some parts of the United States, it is not complete until the tenant vacates within a reasonable time.
    IV. Generally, the acts must be of such serious and permanent character as to deny the tenant the enjoyment of his possessing rights.
    V. In this event, upon abandonment of the premises, the tenant's liability for that ceases.
    The CORRECT answer is:
    A. II, I, IV, III, V
    B. V, II, III, I, IV
    C. IV, III, I, II, V
    D. I, III, V, IV, II

    1.____

2. I. The powerlessness before private and public authorities that is the typical experience of the slum tenant is reminiscent of the situation of blue-collar workers all through the nineteenth century.
    II. Similarly, in recent years, this chapter of history has been reopened by anti-poverty groups which have attempted to organize slum tenants to enable them to bargain collectively with their landlords about the conditions of their tenancies.
    III. It is familiar history that many of the worker remedied their condition by joining together and presenting their demands collectively.
    IV. Like the workers, tenants are forced by the conditions of modern life into substantial dependence on these who possess great political aid and economic power.
    V. What's more, the very fact of dependence coupled with an absence of education and self-confidence makes them hesitant and unable to stand up for what they need from those in power.
    The CORRECT answer is:
    A. V, IV, I, II, III
    B. II, III, I, V, IV
    C. III, I, V, IV, II
    D. I, IV, V, III, II

    2.____

3. I. A railroad, for example, when not acting as a common carrier may contract away responsibility for its own negligence.
    II. As to a landlord, however, no decision has been found relating to the legal effect of a clause shifting the statutory duty of repair to the tenant.
    III. The courts have not passed on the validity of clauses relieving the landlord of this duty and liability.
    IV. They have, however, upheld the validity of exculpatory clauses in other types of contracts.

    3.____

145

V. Housing regulations impose a duty upon the landlord to maintain leased premises in safe condition.
VI. As another example, a bailee may limit his liability except for gross negligence, willful acts, or fraud.

The CORRECT answer is:
A. II, I, VI, IV, III, V
B. I, III, IV, V, VI, II
C. III, V, I, IV, II, VI
D. V, III, IV, I, VI, II

4.
I. Since there are only samples in the building, retail or consumer sales are generally eschewed by mart occupants, and in some instances, rigid controls are maintained to limit entrance to the mart only to those persons engaged in retailing.
II. Since World War I, in many larger cities, there has developed a new type of property, called the mart building.
III. It can, therefore, be used by wholesalers and jobbers for the display of sample merchandise.
IV. This type of building is most frequently a multi-storied, finished interior property which is a cross between a retail arcade and a loft building.
V. This limitation enables the mart occupants to ship the orders from another location after the retailer or dealer makes his selection from the samples.

The CORRECT answer is:
A. II, IV, III, I, V
B. IV, III, V, I, II
C. I, III, II, IV, V
D. I, IV, II, III, V

5.
I. In general, staff-line friction reduces the distinctive contribution of staff personnel.
II. The conflicts, however, introduce an uncontrolled element into the managerial system.
III. On the other hand, the natural resistance of the line to staff innovations probably usefully restrains over-eager efforts to apply untested procedures on a large scale.
IV. Under such conditions, it is difficult to know when valuable ideas are being sacrificed.
V. The relatively weak position of staff, requiring accommodation to the line, tends to restrict their ability to engage in free, experimental innovation.

The CORRECT answer is:
A. IV, II, III, I, V
B. I, V, III, II, IV
C. V, III, I, II, IV
D. II, I, IV, V, III

KEY (CORRECT ANSWERS)

1. A
2. D
3. D
4. A
5. B

TEST 3

DIRECTIONS: Questions 1 through 4 consist of six sentences which can be arranged in a logical sequence. For each question, select the choice which places the numbered sentences in the MOST logical sequent. *PRINT THE LETTER OF THE CORRECT ANSWER IN THE SPACE AT THE RIGHT.*

1. I. The burden of proof as to each issue is determined before trial and remains upon the same party throughout the trial.
    II. The jury is at liberty to believe one witness' testimony as against a number of contradictory witnesses.
    III. In a civil case, the party bearing the burden of proof is required to prove his contention by a fair preponderance of the evidence.
    IV. However, it must be noted that a fair preponderance of evidence does not necessarily mean a greater number of witnesses.
    V. The burden of proof is the burden which rests upon one of the parties to an action to persuade the trier of the facts, generally the jury, that a proposition he asserts is true.
    VI. If the evidence is equally balanced, or if it leaves the jury in such doubt as to be unable to decide the controversy either way, judgment must be given against the party upon whom the burden of proof rests.
    The CORRECT answer is:
    A. III, II, V, IV, I, VI   B. I, II, VI, V, III, IV
    C. III, IV, V, I, II, VI   D. V, I, III, VI, IV, II

    1.____

2. I. If a parent is without assets and is unemployed, he cannot be convicted of the crime of non-support of a child.
    II. The term "sufficient ability" has been held to mean sufficient financial ability.
    III. It does not matter if his unemployment is by choice or unavoidable circumstances.
    IV. If he fails to take any steps at all, he may be liable to prosecution for endangering the welfare of a child.
    V. Under the penal law, a parent is responsible for the support of his minor child only if the parent is "of sufficient ability."
    VI. An indigent parent may meet his obligation by borrowing money or by seeking aid under the provisions of the Social Welfare Law.
    The CORRECT answer is:
    A. VI, I, V, III, II, IV   B. I, III, V, II, IV, VI
    C. V, II, I, III, VI, IV   D. I, VI, IV, V, II, III

    2.____

3. I. Consider, for example, the case of a rabble rouser who urges a group of twenty people to go out and break the windows of a nearby factory.
    II. Therefore, the law fills the indicated gap with the crime of inciting to riot.
    III. A person is considered guilty of inciting to riot when he urges ten or more persons to engage in tumultuous and violent conduct of a kind likely to create public alarm.
    IV. However, if he has not obtained the cooperation of at least four people, he cannot be charged with unlawful assembly.

    3.____

147

V. The charge of inciting to riot was added to the law to cover types of conduct which cannot be classified as either the crime of "riot" or the crime of "unlawful assembly."
VI. If he acquires the acquiescence of at least four of them, he is guilty of unlawful assembly even if the project does not materialize.

The CORRECT answer is:
- A. III, V, I, VI, IV, II
- B. V, I, IV, VI, II, III
- C. III, IV, I, V, II, VI
- D. V, I, IV, VI, III, II

4. I. If, however, the rebuttal evidence presents an issue of credibility, it is for the jury to determine whether the presumption has, in fact, been destroyed.
    II. Once sufficient evidence to the contrary is introduced, the presumption disappears from the trial.
    III. The effect of a presumption is to place the burden upon the adversary to come forward with evidence to rebut the presumption.
    IV. When a presumption is overcome and ceases to exist in the case, the fact or facts which gave rise to the presumption still remain.
    V. Whether a presumption has been overcome is ordinarily a question for the court.
    VI. Such information may furnish a basis for a logical inference.

The CORRECT answer is:
- A. IV, VI, II, V, I, III
- B. III, II, V, I, IV, VI
- C. V, III, VI, IV, II, I
- D. V, IV, I, II, VI, III

4.____

KEY (CORRECT ANSWERS)

1. D
2. C
3. A
4. B